The Supper Book

'Life is too short to stuff a mushroom'
Shirley Conran

Elizabeth Kent

The Supper Book

Illustrations by David Green

Sidgwick & Jackson
London

For my parents

First published in Great Britain in 1982
by Sidgwick & Jackson Limited
Copyright © 1982 Elizabeth Kent

ISBN 0-283-98830-4

Filmset by Coats Dataprint Limited, Smithton, Inverness,
and printed in Great Britain by
A. H. Wheaton of Exeter
for Sidgwick & Jackson Limited
1 Tavistock Chambers, Bloomsbury Way
London WC1A 2SG

For permission to reprint recipes first published in
Country Cuisine I would like to thank Sam
Chalmers at Le Talbooth for *Turkey in Green
Waistcoats*; Colin White at White's Restaurant for
White's Moussaka; Ian MacKenzie at Lamb's
Restaurant for *Pork with Cider and Spices*; Joyce
Molyneux and Tom Jaine at The Carved Angel
for *Creamy Veal with Carrots*; Nigel and Sue
McKenzie at The Hungry Monk for *Banoffi Pie*;
Ralph Vivian Neal and Graham Cornish at Well
House for *Brown Bread Ice-cream*; Robert
Greenstock for *Dorset Apple Cake*; Catherine and
Nicholas Healey at Dunderry Lodge for *Irish Soda
Bread*. The idea for *Ricotta and Vegetable Custard* was
derived from a recipe by Joe Famularo.

Special thanks to Mary Jane Coles
for the prolonged use of her kitchen.

Symbols

◖ the approximate time it takes to prepare all the ingredients according to the instructions in the list of ingredients and in the method, up to the stage where any cooking is involved.

◉ the approximate time it takes to cook the dish, either on top of the stove or under the grill or, where indicated, in the oven. Not included is the time it may take to reheat a dish if it has been partially prepared ahead.

◐ recipes which can successfully be fully or partially prepared up to twenty-four hours before they are needed. Such recipes should be reheated very gently, if they are to be served hot.

◒ recipes which can successfully be fully or partially prepared up to two hours before they are to be eaten. Again, if they have to be reheated, this should be done very gently.

▲▲ dishes which are ideal for storing in the freezer

✱ recipes which are both quick and easy to make.

Measurements

All spoon measurements are both standard and level. Where 'level' is specified, this is for emphasis only.

Contents

Introduction

Supper is an unpretentious meal. Eaten almost every evening of the week, it must be adaptable, relaxed and place no strain on the cook.

There are plenty of cookbooks which cater for dinner-party cooking, yet there are few which concentrate on supper, the meal we cook most frequently. As a result, we tend either to cook a well-tried favourite or to search through half a dozen books for a recipe that suits the time and ingredients available.

This book attempts to fill the gap by providing *nothing but* delicious, uncomplicated recipes for supper. Because it is a capricious meal – the result of whim as well as the more pressing demands of time, economy and hunger – the choice has been made as wide as possible. This should eliminate the most difficult part of cooking supper every day – deciding what to cook. There are recipes for every conceivable supper, from an omelette in front of the telly, to hamburgers in the garden, or moussaka for friends at the weekend. Preparation and cooking times at the end of each recipe show at a glance which dishes can be made at the last minute, a few hours ahead or the day before.

The criteria used in choosing the recipes were that they should be imaginative, inexpensive and simple to prepare. All the ingredients can be found in any supermarket. Most of the recipes are so easy that they could be eaten within an hour of walking in the door. Those which take longer – like lasagne, cannelloni or Virginia baked ham – are included because they are such favourites and ideal for an informal supper party.

While supper is a simple meal, it doesn't necessarily consist of just one main course. In hot weather, you may prefer two lighter ones – perhaps salad or fish with homemade ice-cream to follow. Each recipe (excluding the side salads, a few rice dishes, the puddings and pies chapters) could be a supper in itself. But the book is designed so that, if you felt hungrier, it would be easy to supplement the dish with recipes from other parts of the book. The desserts are meant to perk up a meal that is virtuously using up leftovers. The storecupboard chapter is for suppers that must, by necessity, be constructed from the contents of the freezer or larder shelf. Lists at the back give recipes that are particularly suitable for large numbers, slimmers, children or supper parties.

The Supper Book, I hope, offers dishes which, in time, will spring to mind just as quickly as the old favourites. It should help you spend less time searching for recipes and more time enjoying them. Above all, *The Supper Book* is written for those who love good food and who would like to eat well every night of the year.

Main Course Soups

Most soups are too hearty to be starters – they satisfy the appetite too efficiently. Even a delicate vichyssoise leaves little room for the lamb chops.

As a main course, soup can be thoroughly indulged. It makes a perfect one-pot meal, needing only bread and cheese to round it off. Always versatile, it can be hustled into a thermos for a picnic supper, downed in front of the telly or put into a mug for drinking atop a stepladder. For those too tired to cook or too busy to eat, it is a godsend.

When feeding ravenous carnivores (determined to get their pound of flesh), raid an international larder. Try Hungarian goulash soup – thick with meat, tomatoes and hint of caraway. A *soupe de poisson* or modest *bouillabaisse* would quell most hunger pangs – as would the fish chowders so popular in America. These can all be made with local ingredients and are by no means 'exotic' or difficult.

There is still a lot of poppycock talked about the necessity of homemade stock for soup. If you have the time and the ingredients to make stock, do. If not, substitute a stock cube and don't feel guilty about it. (If chefs like Michel Guérard can advocate using them, they can't be doing our tastebuds much harm.) But do choose a good one (Knorr and Maggi are, to my mind, the best) and use it with discretion.

A recipe for soup is useful but certainly not mandatory. It is immensely satisfying to make it *ad hoc*, out of 'nothing'. When making soup from odds and ends in the larder, don't liquidize it unless the vegetables are roughly the same colour. Otherwise the result will be murky green sludge. Leftover cooked meats are a good way of plumping up a soup but adding cooked vegetables is not successful. Their best flavour, colour and texture have gone into the first cooking and your soup will not recapture them. All soups mature if left for a few hours or overnight – those with cream should be refrigerated and reheated with care.

In the unlikely event of the soup going wrong, there is always a way to rescue it. A soup which appears too thin can be thickened at the last minute with a little *crème fraîche* or two egg yolks mixed with single or double cream (in either case, mix a little of the hot soup into the cold mixture before whisking it all in and then take care that it doesn't boil). A *beurre manié* (page 38) whisked, small bits at a time, into the soup will also help to thicken it. If, in a moment of absent-mindedness, you oversalt the soup – add a small potato to it and this will absorb the saltiness. A little lemon juice will sharpen the flavour; a generous grating of nutmeg or ground coriander will add character; a pinch of sugar will remove any bitterness; and a little chopped watercress will give the soup 'bite'.

7

Manhattan Clam Chowder

In New York, they like their chowders rich and russet-coloured; in New England, the tomatoes are replaced by cream and milk.

1 oz (25g) butter
6 oz (175g) streaky bacon, rind removed and diced
6 oz (175g) finely chopped onion
4 carrots, peeled and finely chopped
2 stalks celery, finely diced
2 tablespoons chopped fresh parsley
2 14-oz (400g) tins Italian tomatoes
2 medium tins clams in brine, giving 6 oz (175g) drained weight
salt and pepper
1 level teaspoon dried thyme
1/2 small bay leaf
1 large potato, peeled and finely diced

Melt the butter in a large saucepan and, when foaming, add the bacon. Stir until well coated in the butter then leave to cook until it darkens in colour. Add the onion and cook until soft and transparent. Add the carrots, celery and parsley and cook over low heat for about 10 minutes, stirring from time to time. Drain the tomatoes and pour their juice into a measuring jug. Tip the tomatoes into the pan and break them up with the side of a wooden spoon. Drain the clams, adding their liquid to the tomato juice. Add enough water to bring the liquid in the jug up to 2 pints (1.1 litres) and pour into the saucepan. Add a good seasoning of salt and freshly ground black pepper, the thyme and bay leaf. Bring up to the boil and stir, then reduce the heat and simmer, partly covered, for 45 minutes. Add the potato, cover and cook gently for 30 minutes. Finally, add the clams and simmer for 15 minutes longer. Check for seasoning and scoop out the bay leaf. Serve at once or reheat when needed.

Serves 6–8

 ⬤ 15 minutes   ▣ 1³/4 hours   ◀

Hungarian Goulash Soup

Serve this on a blustery evening with dark rye bread, unsalted butter and lashings of cream cheese.

1 oz (25g) butter and 1 tablespoon oil *or* 3 tablespoons bacon fat
1/2 lb (225g) stewing or braising steak, cut into chunks
1 medium onion, peeled and sliced
1 small green pepper, finely chopped
1 level tablespoon flour
2 level teaspoons paprika
1 1/2 pints (850ml) beef stock
1 14-oz (400g) tin Italian tomatoes
1 small clove of garlic, crushed
good pinch of chilli powder
1/4 teaspoon caraway seeds
salt and pepper
soured cream to garnish (optional)

Heat the butter and oil (or bacon fat) in a large saucepan and brown the meat quickly. Lift out with a slotted spoon and put to one side. Add the onion and pepper to the pan and cook over a moderate heat until the onion is golden. Stir in the flour and paprika and cook for a minute. Remove from the heat and gradually blend in the stock. Return to the heat and add the tomatoes, breaking them up with the side of a wooden spoon. Put the meat back into the pan with the crushed garlic, chilli powder, caraway seeds and a good seasoning of salt and pepper. Simmer partly covered for 1–1 1/2 hours or until the meat is very tender. Check the seasoning and adjust if necessary. Garnish with a swirl of soured cream and serve.

Serves 4

 ⬤ 10 minutes   ▣ 1 1/4 hours   ◀

Tuscan Minestrone

2 oz (50g) butter
4 oz (100g) streaky bacon
 rashers
1 medium onion, peeled and
 chopped
2 large carrots, peeled and
 diced
1 clove of garlic, crushed
1/2 lb (225g) white cabbage,
 finely shredded
1/2 lb (225g) French beans *or*
 sliced courgettes

2 1/2 pints (1.4 litres) chicken
 stock or water
1 14-oz (400g) tin Italian
 tomatoes
2 tablespoons tomato purée
1 teaspoon sugar
1 teaspoon finely chopped
 basil (fresh or dried)
2 1/2 oz (65g) short macaroni
 or broken spaghetti
salt and pepper
grated Parmesan cheese

Melt half the butter in a large, heavy pan. Remove the rind, then chop the bacon into medium dice. Add to the pan and cook until almost crisp. Stir in the onion and continue cooking until pale golden. Add the remaining butter with the carrots, garlic and cabbage. Cover with a piece of buttered paper and leave them to steam gently for about 10 minutes, shaking the pan occasionally to prevent sticking. Remove the paper, then add the beans or courgettes, stock, tomatoes and their juice, tomato purée, sugar and basil. Break up the tomatoes with the side of a wooden spoon and stir until the mixture is well blended. Partly cover and simmer gently for 45 minutes. Add the pasta with a good seasoning of salt and pepper, then simmer partly covered for a further 40–50 minutes. Stir in a rounded tablespoon of grated Parmesan, then check the seasoning and adjust if necessary. Serve piping hot with lots of crusty bread and grated Parmesan.

Serves 4–6

🥄 20 minutes   ◙ about 1 3/4 hours   ◕

Basil's Chicken Soup

2 large chicken breasts
2 chicken stock cubes
2 1/2 pints (1.4 litres) boiling
 water
sprig of parsley, scrap of bay
 leaf, few peppercorns
1 oz (25g) butter
1 medium onion, peeled and
 chopped

3 large carrots (about 1/2
 lb/225g), peeled and finely
 diced
1 tablespoon finely chopped
 parsley
6 oz (175g) *petits pois* (frozen
 are best for colour)
2 oz (50g) dried tagliatelle
salt and pepper

Skin the chicken breasts, then put them into a large saucepan. Dissolve the stock cubes in the boiling water and pour into the pan. Add the parsley, bay leaf and peppercorns, then bring to the boil. Reduce the heat, cover and simmer until the chicken is tender (about 30 minutes). Lift the chicken out and sieve the liquid through a fine mesh into a jug. Remove the chicken bones and chop the flesh into medium chunks.

As the chicken cooks, prepare the vegetables. Melt the butter in a large saucepan and, when foaming, add the onion. Cook until soft and translucent, then add the carrots and toss well in the buttery juices. Cover with a buttered paper and cook over low heat for about 10 minutes. Discard the paper.

Pour the stock into the vegetable pan. Bring up to the boil, then reduce the heat and add the chicken chunks and parsley. Simmer uncovered for 15 minutes, then add the peas and tagliatelle (broken into 1 1/2-inch/3.5cm lengths) and simmer for 25 minutes longer. Season well with salt and pepper and serve.

Serves 6

🥄 10 minutes   ◙ 1 1/4 hours   ◕

French Pea Soup

1 oz (25g) butter
1 medium onion, peeled and
  finely chopped
1 oz (25g) flour
1 pint (575ml) chicken stock

1 bunch of watercress
8 large lettuce leaves
1/2 lb (225g) peas
salt and pepper
5–8 fl oz (150–225ml) milk

Melt the butter in a large saucepan. When foaming, add the onion and sauté until soft and transparent. Stir in the flour and cook for a minute. Remove from the heat and blend in the chicken stock gradually. Return to the heat and slowly bring up to the boil.

Rinse the watercress and lettuce thoroughly, then drain. Shred roughly and add to the boiling stock with the peas. Cover, reduce the heat and simmer gently for about 20 minutes. Put the soup, small amounts at a time, in a liquidizer and blend until smooth. Return to the pan and season well with salt and pepper. Stir in enough milk to give a creamy consistency. Gently reheat to just below boiling point. Check the seasoning and serve. (Garnish, if you like, with a dollop of thick cream and finely chopped red-skinned apple.)

Serves 4

🍴 10 minutes ◉ 40 minutes ◕

Sweetcorn Chowder

4 oz (100g) salt pork or
  streaky bacon rashers
2 oz (50g) butter
1 medium onion, peeled and
  finely sliced
2 large stalks celery, diced
1 oz (25g) flour
1 pint (575ml) chicken stock
  or water

3/4 lb (350g) potatoes, peeled
  and cut into medium
  chunks
2 tablespoons chopped parsley
1 12-oz (350g) tin sweetcorn
  kernels
1 pint (575ml) milk
salt and pepper

Remove the skin from the salt pork (or rind from the bacon) and discard. Cut the pork into thin strips, then dice.

Melt half the butter in a large, heavy pan. Add the pork dice and cook until crisp. Add the onion and celery and cook slowly until the onion is golden. Put the remaining butter in the pan and, when melted, stir in the flour. Cook for a minute, then remove from the heat and stir in half the stock or water. Return to the heat and stir until it comes to the boil. Simmer gently for several minutes, then add the remaining stock (or water) with the potatoes and half the parsley. Partly cover and simmer gently for about 20 minutes or until the potatoes are tender. Add the sweetcorn (well drained of juice) and 3/4 pint (425ml) of milk. Simmer *very* gently, partly covered, for a further 20 minutes. If it seems very thick, add the remaining milk and reheat gently. Season to taste with salt and black pepper and add the remaining parsley. Serve or keep warm until needed.

Serves 4–6

🍴 10 minutes ◉ 1 hour

Jerusalem Artichoke Soup

A soup of distinctive flavour but, alas, nondescript colour. It needs a last-minute flourish of bacon bits or chopped watercress.

2 lbs (900g) Jerusalem artichokes
2 oz (50g) butter
6 oz (175g) chopped onion
2 rashers unsmoked back bacon, diced
1 small clove of garlic, crushed
1 pint (575ml) chicken stock or water
3/4 pint (425ml) milk
salt and pepper
1 tablespoon chopped parsley

Peel the artichokes (or if you're in a hurry, just give them a good scrub and sieve the soup after liquidizing it).

Melt half the butter in a large, heavy saucepan. Add the onion and bacon and cook until the onion is soft and the bacon almost crisp. Cut the artichokes into thick slices and add to the pan with the remaining butter and crushed garlic. Toss the artichokes carefully in the juices, then cover with a buttered paper and cook over a gentle heat for 15–20 minutes.

Discard the paper, pour in the stock and simmer gently for 20 minutes. Purée the soup in a liquidizer, then return to the pan. Add enough milk (you may need slightly more than 3/4 pint/425ml) to give it a creamy consistency, without being too thick. Season to taste with salt and pepper, then sprinkle with chopped parsley. Reheat slowly and serve (or remove from the heat and keep in a cool place until needed).

Serves 6

 15 minutes ◉ 50 minutes ◀

Leek and Watercress Soup

The watercress adds pep and much-needed colour to the familiar team of leek and potato.

4 large leeks
8 good-sized spring onions
2 oz (50g) butter
3/4 lb (350g) potatoes
1 large bunch of watercress
1 1/4 pints (700ml) chicken stock
1/2 pint (275ml) milk
1/4 pint (150ml) single cream
salt and pepper
chopped chives or spring onion tops to garnish

Cut the leeks in half lengthwise, wash thoroughly and shred. Do the same with the spring onions.

Melt the butter in a large saucepan, then add the leeks and spring onions. Toss well in the butter, then cook for 5–10 minutes, stirring occasionally.

Peel the potatoes and chop into medium dice. Wash the watercress and chop roughly. Add both to the pan with the stock. Cover and cook over moderate heat for 20 minutes or until the potatoes are cooked through. Pour the vegetables and stock, small amounts at a time, into a liquidizer and blend until smooth. Return to the pan and stir in the milk, cream and a good seasoning of salt and pepper. Slowly reheat to just below boiling point. Taste for seasoning and serve. Scatter a few chopped chives or spring onion tops over each bowl.

Serves 6

 15 minutes ◉ 45 minutes

11

Gazpacho

Despite the number of ingredients, this soup is very quick to make. A reliable standby when the temperatures soar.

1 1-lb, 12-oz (793g) tin tomatoes
1 19-oz (540ml) tin tomato juice
2 teaspoons sugar
large pinch of dried thyme
1 teaspoon chopped parsley
3 tablespoons olive oil
2 tablespoons wine vinegar
3 large slices white bread, crusts removed

1 large cucumber
1 green pepper
2 large stalks celery
8 spring onions *or* 1 small onion
1 pint (575ml) chicken stock
1 clove of garlic
salt and black pepper
croûtons and chopped chives

Put the tomatoes, their juice and the tomato juice into a large mixing bowl. Stir in the sugar, thyme, parsley, olive oil and vinegar. Crumble the bread into the bowl and blend in. Chop the cucumber (no need to peel it) into small dice and put half into the mixing bowl. Do the same with the green pepper, celery and spring onions.

Stir the chicken stock into the tomato mixture. Crush the garlic and add. Pour the soup, by thirds, into the liquidizer and blend for a very short time (several seconds only), just long enough to break the vegetables down slightly. Pour into a large bowl, stir in the remaining vegetables and season to taste with salt and freshly ground black pepper. Refrigerate until well chilled, or stir in a few ice-cubes and serve straight away. (Add the croûtons and chives just before serving.)

Serves 8

 30 minutes ◖

12

Whizzo Carrot Soup

This soup has a glorious colour, and a flavour that is equally good hot or cold.

2 oz (50g) butter
1 medium onion, peeled and finely sliced
2 cloves of garlic, crushed
1 1/2 lbs (675g) carrots, peeled and chopped
2 pints (1.1 litres) beef stock

salt and pepper
a little grated nutmeg
1/4 pint (150ml) single cream *or* double cream if serving cold
1 tablespoon finely chopped parsley

Melt half the butter in a large, heavy pan. Add the onion and cook until almost coloured. Add the remaining butter, the garlic and carrots. Toss well in the buttery juices, then cover with a buttered paper and leave to 'sweat' for 10 minutes.

Discard the paper, pour in the stock and bring up to the boil. Reduce the heat, partly cover and simmer gently for 20 minutes. Put the soup through a liquidiser and return to the pan. Season to taste with salt, black pepper and a little grated nutmeg. Heat gently, then stir in the cream (if serving the soup cold, omit this step and fold in the cream, whisked until thick, just before dishing it up). Slowly reheat to just below boiling point. Check the seasoning, then scatter chopped parsley on top and serve.

Serves 4–6

 10 minutes 45 minutes ◖

Mainly Vegetables

Vegetables, which were unpopular for so long, have suddenly become the last word in culinary fashion – and not simply because of their attractive prices.

Much of the credit must go to the propagators of *nouvelle cuisine*. In the twinkling of a *mange-tout*, they have rid vegetables of their wholesome-but-dull image. No longer are they the soggy adjunct to the meat – but ingredients worthy of individual treatment. Improved cooking techniques have made a feature of their colour, texture and flavour. While *terrine des légumes*, *gâteau* of carrots and *feuilleté d'asperges* may be too complicated for the supper table, they do illustrate what delicious potential there is. Furthermore, the same principle – of cooking vegetables with care and imagination – can easily be translated to more modest dishes.

Who is to say, after all, that a *ragoût* must be made with meat? Why not with spring vegetables, cooked in a little stock and finished with a light dusting of cheese, toasted nuts or breadcrumbs? A vegetable stew (cooked quickly instead of the traditional few hours) could be made entirely of green vegetables – broccoli, beans, courgettes – and served with a herby hollandaise. Similarly, cauliflower – too often the victim of a suffocating cheese sauce – deserves better treatment. Try it with a mild curry sauce or coated while still warm with a blend of Dijon mustard and cream. Or sautéed, perhaps, in butter and breadcrumbs or pine nuts until crisp and brown.

As the price of meat rockets, so does the value of vegetables. They become even more important as a means of stretching meat further or as a meal in themselves. A brilliant swede purée can revitalize cold lamb; a *galette* of sausage, cabbage and onion would satisfy the hungriest Rugby forward.

The knack of vegetable cooking lies in varied techniques – none of them difficult. The common carrot needn't automatically be boiled. It could instead be stir-fried, steamed, braised in stock, roasted, puréed, or grated and baked as a custard. The Chinese have always had more respect for the texture of vegetables and their stir-frying technique guarantees that this is not lost during cooking. It's so quick that vegetables which might take twenty minutes to cook in boiling water are done in a quarter that time. Any vegetable that you would cook *al dente* – beans, broccoli, cauliflower, cabbage, carrots, *mange-tout* peas – is suitable for stir-frying. A wok is not essential – any large, heavy frying pan will do. But the vegetables must be sliced beforehand as no time must be lost once the cooking has begun. Very hot stock (no more than ¼ pint/150ml) can be substituted if you would rather not use oil. Different oils – corn, peanut, hazelnut, walnut – will each produce different nuances of flavour.

13

Baked Aubergines
with Tomatoes and Cheese

By grilling rather than frying the aubergines, you retain their shape and use far less oil.

2 medium aubergines
salt
olive or vegetable oil
pepper
4 oz (100g) good Cheddar,
 grated

1 lb (450g) firm ripe tomatoes
6 oz (175g) Mozzarella cheese
a little oregano or marjoram

Rinse the aubergines, wipe dry, then remove the furry ends. Place each aubergine on its side and cut both into thin slices. Put the slices on a double layer of kitchen paper, salt generously and leave for at least half an hour. Then rinse and pat dry (make sure that they are *completely* dry). Arrange the slices on the rack in a grill pan and brush them with oil. Put under the grill and leave until nicely browned. Flip over and do the same for the reverse side. Continue until all the slices have been done.

Cut each slice in half and place them in rows, rounded side up, in a gratin dish. Give a good seasoning of salt and pepper, then scatter the Cheddar cheese evenly on top. Quarter the tomatoes and place, rounded side up, on top of the cheese. Cut the Mozzarella into thin strips and make a lattice pattern over the tomatoes. Give a light dusting of oregano or marjoram, then bake in a preheated oven (375°F/Gas Mark 5/190°C) for 45 minutes or until hot and bubbling. Serve with a crisp green salad.

Serves 4

◖ 45 minutes   ◙ 45 minutes   ◐

14

The Priest Has Fainted
(Imam Bayildi)

So great was his pleasure upon tasting this dish that the eponymous (Turkish) priest swooned with delight.

2 large aubergines
salt
3–4 tablespoons olive or
 vegetable oil
8 oz (225g) chopped onion
1/2 large green pepper,
 chopped
1 clove of garlic, crushed

1 lb (450g) ripe tomatoes,
 roughly chopped
1 teaspoon sugar
1/2 teaspoon cinnamon
1 tablespoon raisins
2 tablespoons chopped fresh
 parsley
pepper

Halve the aubergines, score with a knife and sprinkle generously with salt. Leave sandwiched between two plates with a weight on top for at least 30 minutes. Then rinse the aubergines and dry with kitchen paper. Scoop out the flesh, leaving an 1/8-inch (.25cm) border all the way round, and chop roughly.

Heat 2 tablespoons of oil in a large, heavy pan and cook the onion, green pepper and garlic for 5–10 minutes. Add a little more oil and the aubergine chunks. Cook, stirring occasionally, until the aubergine is lightly browned. Add the tomatoes, sugar, cinnamon, raisins and half the parsley and cook for a further 5 minutes. Season well with salt and pepper.

Put the aubergine shells in a shallow baking tin. Brush the inside of the shells with oil and season with salt and pepper. Pile the tomato mixture into the shells and top with the remaining parsley. Bake in the centre of a preheated oven (350°F/Gas Mark 4/180°C) for 30–40 minutes. Take out and serve warm with fluffy white rice and a green salad.

Serves 4

◖ 40 minutes   ◙ 25 minutes + 35 minutes (oven)   ◐

Gratin of Ham, New Potatoes and Leeks

1 lb (450g) new potatoes	1/2 pint (275ml) milk
1 1/2 lbs (675g) leeks	2 oz (50g) Cheddar, grated
3 oz (75g) butter	1 tablespoon chopped parsley
salt and pepper	*or* chervil
2 oz (50g) flour	4 large slices cooked ham, off
1/2 pint (275ml) chicken stock	the bone

Scrub the potatoes, boil until just tender, then drain well. Clean the leeks thoroughly, chop into thick slices, then put into a saucepan with 1 oz (25g) butter and a good seasoning of salt and pepper. Cover and cook over a low heat (shaking the pan occasionally to prevent sticking) until tender.

As the vegetables cook, prepare the sauce. Melt the remaining butter in a large, heavy saucepan and stir in the flour. Cook for a minute or two, then take off the heat and gradually blend in the stock and milk. Return to the heat and stir until the mixture boils. Simmer gently for several minutes, add the cheese and parsley, then season to taste with salt and pepper.

Divide the leek mixture and their buttery juices between the ham slices, putting a good dollop down the middle of each. Then roll up carefully and place at intervals in a large, buttered gratin dish. Slice the potatoes in half and place in between and around the ham. Pour the sauce over, making sure it gets to the bottom of the dish. Cover with foil until needed, then bake (uncovered) near the top of a preheated oven (350°F/Gas Mark 4/180°C) for 35–45 minutes or until golden brown.

Serves 4

⬇ 10 minutes ◼ 20 minutes + 40 minutes (oven) ◑ ▲▲

Scalloped Potatoes with Ham

Sweet potatoes are yams with a wrinkled brown skin and flaming orange interior.

1 1/2 lbs (675g) sweet potatoes	2 spring onions, chopped
1 1/2 lbs (675g) ordinary potatoes	1 pint (575ml) milk
2 tablespoons soft butter	salt and black pepper
2 level tablespoons plain flour	2 tablespoons soft brown sugar
1 level tablespoon dry mustard	chopped parsley *or* chervil
4 large slices honey roast ham (about 1/2 lb/225g), shredded	(fresh or dried)
	1 1/2 tablespoons butter

Peel both sets of potatoes and cut into thin slices. Rinse well, then drain and pat dry with kitchen paper or a tea towel.

Mix the soft butter with the flour and dry mustard until you have a smooth paste. Put a layer of white potatoes (roughly half) in the bottom of a large, lightly buttered gratin dish. Scatter half the ham and spring onions on top. Dot with bits of the butter mixture (using half of it) and cover with milk. Season well with salt and freshly ground black pepper.

Make an identical layer on top, then a final layer of sweet potatoes (using them all). Season generously with salt and pepper, sprinkle with brown sugar and chopped parsley or chervil. Then dot with the remaining butter. Cover loosely with foil and bake in the centre of a preheated oven (350°F/Gas Mark 4/180°C) for 1 hour, then remove the foil and bake for a further 30–45 minutes or until the top is lightly browned. (If the mixture starts to bubble furiously during the first hour, turn the temperature down slightly.)

Serves 6

⬇ 30 minutes ◼ 1 1/2–2 hours

15

Potatoes in Dinner Jackets

Posh jacket potatoes – dressed up with blue cheese, bacon and soured cream. At their best hot but could also be eaten cold.

2 large potatoes
1/2 oz (15g) soft butter
3 oz (75g) German blue Brie or mild Stilton, rind removed
2 back bacon rashers, cooked until crisp

3 oz (75ml) soured cream
salt and black pepper
chopped chives *or* parsley to garnish

Scrub the potatoes well and prick in several places with a fork. If you have thin skewers, stick one into the centre of each potato (this helps them to cook evenly). Put the potatoes into a hot oven (400°F/Gas Mark 6/200°C) for about 1¹/₄ hours or until the potatoes are cooked through.

Take out and as soon as they are cool enough to handle (a few minutes, don't let them get cold), slice each potato in half lengthwise. Scoop out most of the flesh, leaving a thin border next to the skin. Mash the potato well, then mash in the butter, blue cheese, well crumbled bacon and soured cream. (The mixture should now be smooth but quite thick.) Season well with salt and pepper. Pile the potato back into the shells (piling it up slightly in the centre) and dust lightly with chopped chives or parsley.* Place in a shallow baking tin and put on the second shelf from the top of a preheated oven (425°F/Gas Mark 7/220°C). Bake for 20–25 minutes or until the potatoes are piping hot and lightly browned. Take out and allow to cool slightly, then serve with a crunchy vegetable or green salad.

Serves 4

◗ 5 minutes   ▣ 1³/₄ hours   ◕ to *

16

Soufflé Potatoes

2 large potatoes
2 oz (50g) butter
4 button onions or shallots, peeled and quartered
4 oz (100g) button mushrooms, diced

salt and pepper
2 egg yolks
3 oz (75g) Cheddar, grated
generous pinch of dry mustard
generous grating of nutmeg
2 egg whites

Put the potatoes into a hot oven (400°F/Gas Mark 6/200°C) and bake until tender (1¹/₄–1¹/₂ hours).

While they're cooking, melt 1/2 oz (15g) of butter in a medium saucepan and add the onions. Cook over a moderate heat, stirring from time to time, until they are golden. Add another ounce (25g) of butter with the mushrooms and continue cooking until the mushrooms have softened. Season well with salt and pepper and put to one side.

When the potatoes are cooked, take them out and leave for a few minutes or until cool enough to handle. Then cut in half lengthwise and scoop out the potato. Put into a bowl and mash until free of lumps. Mash in the remaining butter, egg yolks and Cheddar with the dry mustard and nutmeg. Season to taste with salt and black pepper. Whisk the egg whites until stiff, then carefully fold into the potato. Pile the mixture back into the skins (which you have put on a shallow baking tray) and return to the hot oven for 20–30 minutes or until golden brown. Take out and serve at once.

Serves 4, or 2 ravenous eaters

◗ 10 minutes   ▣ 1³/₄ hours

Ricotta and Vegetable Custard

This is a singular treat for the tastebuds. The vermouth remains only as the merest suggestion – but how seductive!

1 oz (25g) unsalted butter
8 large pickling onions or shallots, peeled and halved
1 large carrot, peeled and diced
1 large leek, well rinsed and chopped
1/2 lb (225g) *petits pois*
2 1/2 fl oz (65ml) dry vermouth
1/2 lb (225g) ricotta cheese (failing that, sieved cottage cheese)
6 large eggs, lightly beaten
1 level tablespoon flour
2 oz (50g) grated Parmesan
8 fl oz (225ml) double cream
salt and pepper to taste

Melt the butter in a large, heavy saucepan or sauté pan. Add the onions and cook until soft and transparent, stirring from time to time. Add the carrot and leek, cover and cook gently until tender. Add the peas and vermouth and bring to the boil. Reduce the heat and simmer, uncovered, for 5 minutes.*

Put the ricotta into a large mixing bowl and gradually mix in the beaten eggs. Blend in the flour and Parmesan, then the cream (or do this all in a food processor). Season to taste with salt and pepper. Add the vegetables and their liquid and, when well blended, transfer to large, lightly buttered gratin dish (or square baking dish, no more than 2 inches/5cm deep). Bake near the top of a preheated oven (375°F/Gas Mark 5/190°C) for 20–30 minutes or until golden and set (but not dry). Take out and serve warm. (Any left over can be successfully reheated if covered with foil.)

Serves 6

━ 15 minutes ◉ 20 minutes + 25 minutes (oven) ◓ to *

Vegetable Ragoût with Yogurt Sauce

1 small aubergine
4 courgettes
salt
2–4 tablespoons olive or vegetable oil
1 oz (25g) butter
1 small onion, peeled and sliced
4 carrots, peeled and cut into thin strips
4 small leeks, cut into 2-inch (5cm) lengths
1/4 pint (150ml) chicken stock
pepper
1/4 pint (150ml) natural yogurt
2 tablespoons double cream
2 tablespoons grated Parmesan
1 tablespoon chopped parsley

Slice the aubergine and courgettes, salt generously and leave for 30 minutes. Rinse and wipe dry with kitchen paper. Heat 2 tablespoons of oil in a large, heavy sauté pan and cook the courgettes (in batches if necessary, don't crowd the pan), then the aubergine, until lightly browned on both sides (adding more oil as you need it). Lift out with a slotted spoon and put to one side.

Leave about 1 tablespoon of oil in the pan and add the butter. Sauté the onion slices until golden, then add the carrots and leeks. Cover and 'sweat' for 5 minutes, then pour in the stock and cook, partly covered, until the carrots are just tender. Return the courgettes and aubergine to the pan and season well with salt and pepper. Cook gently until the mixture is piping hot.*

Take 1 tablespoon of hot stock from the pan and mix it in a small bowl with the yogurt and double cream. Transfer the vegetables and their juice to a large gratin dish and pour the yogurt sauce down the middle. Scatter the Parmesan and parsley on top and put into a hot oven until the sauce is warm and the cheese has melted. Take out and serve at once.

Serves 4

━ 35 minutes ◉ 40 minutes + 10 minutes (oven) ◓ to *

Winter Vegetable Purée

This may look like hard work but the result – a brilliant trio of contrasting colour and taste – is worth the effort.

1¼ lbs (550g) swede
1½ lbs (675g) carrots
½ pint (275ml) chicken stock
generous pinches of cinnamon or nutmeg, dry mustard and sugar
5 oz (150g) good Cheddar, grated

3 tablespoons single cream
2½ oz (65g) butter
salt and black pepper
1 large onion, peeled and sliced
½ lb (225g) peas
chopped parsley

Peel and chop the swede and carrots, then place in two separate pots. Divide the chicken stock between them, cover and cook until tender. Liquidize each separately, adding any liquid remaining in the pan and, to each one, good pinches of cinnamon, mustard, sugar, 1½ oz (40g) cheese, cream (1 tablespoon for the swede, 2 for the carrots), salt and pepper.

As the vegetables cook, melt 1½ oz (40g) butter in a heavy pan. Sauté the onion slices slowly until pale golden. Add the peas, cover with a buttered paper and cook for 5 minutes.

Lightly butter a round, glass baking dish about 7½ inches (19cm) wide and 3 inches (7.5cm) deep. Spread the swede purée evenly over the bottom, then cover with the onions, peas and their juice and, finally, a layer of the carrot purée. Scatter chopped parsley and the remaining cheese on top. Put into a preheated oven (350°F/Gas Mark 4/180°C) and bake for 20–25 minutes or until piping hot (or cover and bake later). Any leftover purée can be reheated gently.

Serves 4–6

🍂 20 minutes   ▣ 20 minutes + 25 minutes (oven)   ◀

Cauliflower with Curry Cream Sauce

1 very large or 2 medium cauliflower
2 tablespoons toasted walnuts or hazelnuts, chopped

1 tablespoon chopped parsley

Sauce

1½ oz (40g) butter
3 oz (75g) finely chopped onion
2 teaspoons mild curry powder
1 oz (25g) flour
1 teaspoon tomato purée
½ pint (275ml) chicken stock

¼ pint (150ml) milk
2 tablespoons peach or mango chutney
¼ pint (150ml) single cream
good squeeze of lemon juice
salt and pepper

Start by making the sauce. Melt ½ oz (15g) of butter in a medium saucepan and add the onion. Cook, stirring occasionally, until translucent. Add the curry powder and cook for 1 minute, stirring to prevent it burning. Add the remaining butter and stir in the flour. Cook for a minute, then blend in the tomato purée. Take off the heat and gradually blend in the stock and milk. Put over moderate heat, add the chutney and slowly bring up to the boil. Simmer gently for a few minutes, then add the cream, lemon juice, salt and pepper. Keep over a very low heat.*

Break the cauliflower into even-sized florets and boil in a small amount of salted water until *al dente*. Drain well, then arrange in a large gratin dish. Cover with the curry sauce, then scatter the walnuts and parsley on top. Cover and leave until needed – or put straight into a preheated oven (375°F/Gas Mark 5/190°C) for 20–30 minutes (until it is bubbling and lightly browned).

Serves 4–6

🍂 5–10 minutes   ▣ 25 minutes + 25 minutes (oven)   ◑ to *

Sausage and Toasted Cauliflower

1 large cauliflower	1^1/$_2$ teaspoons Dijon mustard
8 large, good old-fashioned sausages	^{1}/$_4$ pint (150ml) double cream
1 oz (25g) butter	3 tablespoons Cheddar, grated
salt and black pepper	4 tablespoons chopped fresh parsley

Separate the cauliflower into florets and put into a large saucepan with a small amount of salted water. Cover and steam quickly until the cauliflower is just tender. Drain very well and put to one side.

As the cauliflower cooks, grill the sausages. When they're crisp and brown, put on a plate and keep warm. Reserve the sausage fat.

Take a few tablespoons of the sausage fat and melt it with half the butter in a large frying pan. Sauté half the cauliflower until lightly browned, then add the remaining butter and sauté the rest. Put the sausages in a diagonal row down one side of a large gratin or baking dish. Arrange the cauliflower down the other side and season well with salt and pepper.

Mix the mustard with the cream and pour into a small pan. Simmer for a minute, then stir in half the grated cheese and half the parsley. Season lightly with salt and pepper. Pour over the cauliflower and top with the remaining cheese and parsley. Bake in a preheated oven (375°F/Gas Mark 5/190°C) for about 20 minutes or until piping hot. Serve with a crisp green vegetable or salad.

Serves 4

◗ 10 minutes ◙ 20 minutes + 20 minutes (oven)

Roast Jerusalem Artichokes with Leeks and Bacon

1 oz (25g) butter	6 leeks, well rinsed and halved lengthwise
3 rashers back bacon, finely diced	^{1}/$_4$ pint (150ml) chicken stock
1 lb (450g) Jerusalem artichokes, well scrubbed but not peeled	salt and black pepper

Melt the butter in a large flameproof gratin dish and cook the bacon in it until almost crisp. Slice the artichokes thickly and add to the pan. Toss in the buttery juices and cook for about 5 minutes. Chop the leeks roughly and add to the pan with the chicken stock. Mix the vegetables carefully until well moistened with the stock, then season well with salt and pepper. Put into a preheated oven (375°F/Gas Mark 5/190°C) and bake for an hour, basting from time to time. (Test the artichokes after 45 minutes – they should be tender but not mushy.)

Serves 2

◗ 10 minutes ◙ 10 minutes + 1 hour (oven)

Vegetable Linguine
with Spring Onion Sauce

Prettier than pasta, and with fewer calories.

1 lb (450g) carrots, peeled
1 lb (450g) courgettes
1/2 pint (275ml) chicken stock
1/2 oz (15g) butter
1 large or 2 small spring
  onions, finely chopped

3 rounded tablespoons cream
  cheese
salt, black pepper
chopped parsley (fresh or
  dried) to garnish

Cut the carrots and courgettes into very thin strips, about 3 inches/7cm long. Heat the chicken stock in a large saucepan. Add first the carrots, then the courgettes. Partly cover and boil rapidly for 5–8 minutes, or until the vegetables are *al dente*.

As they cook, melt the butter in a small saucepan. Sauté the spring onions until soft, then add the cream cheese. Stir with a wooden spoon until it has melted.

Drain the carrots and courgettes, reserving the stock left in the pan. Return the vegetables to the pan, cover and keep warm. Add enough of the stock to the cream cheese to make a smooth creamy sauce. Season to taste with salt and black pepper. Tip over the hot vegetables, scraping out with a spatula and toss carefully. Give a light dusting of parsley and serve at once.

Serves 2–3

◗ 10 minutes   ▣ 10 minutes   ✻

20

Stir-fried Cabbage
with Fennel and Sausage

1 oz (25g) butter
1 tablespoon olive or vegetable
  oil
1 medium onion, peeled and
  sliced
1 small white cabbage, finely
  shredded

1 large fennel bulb, finely
  shredded
1 1/2 teaspoons fennel seeds
1/2 pint (275ml) chicken stock
salt and black pepper
8 large sausages
chopped chervil or parsley

Melt the butter and oil in a large sauté pan. Add the onion and cook until just about to turn colour. Add the cabbage, fennel and fennel seeds. Stir-fry over a fairly high heat for several minutes. Pour in the chicken stock, partly cover and cook rapidly for about 8 minutes (until the cabbage and fennel are tender but not soft). Remove the lid and boil quickly until most of the liquid has evaporated. Season with salt and pepper.

While the vegetables cook, grill the sausages until crisp and brown. Transfer to a plate and keep warm.

Tip the contents of the vegetable pan (with any juices) into a hot serving dish. Place the sausages in a diagonal row down the middle (or slice them diagonally into large chunks and mix into the cabbage) and scatter chopped chervil or parsley over the top. Serve on its own or with creamy mashed potatoes.

Serves 4

◗ 10 minutes   ▣ about 20 minutes   ◖

Field Mushroom Croustades

2 wholemeal croustades (page 118) or toast
2 oz (50g) butter
2 tablespoons dry sherry or brandy
10 oz (275g) flat mushrooms, thickly sliced
salt and pepper
5 oz (150ml) soured cream
chopped parsley or chervil

Put the croustades or toast on ovenproof plates and into a moderate oven to warm through.

Heat the butter with the sherry (or brandy) in a large, heavy sauté or frying pan. When hot, add the mushrooms and a light seasoning of salt and pepper. Cook quickly until the mushrooms have darkened in colour and softened slightly. Lift them out with a slotted spoon and keep warm.

Boil the juices in the pan rapidly for a minute, then remove from the heat and whisk in all but 1 tablespoon of the soured cream. When well blended, fold in the mushrooms and their juice. Transfer quickly to the croustades. Top with swirls of the remaining soured cream and a light dusting of chopped parsley or chervil. Serve at once.

Serves 2

5 minutes ◙ 5–7 minutes ✱

SC - B✱

Ragoût of Lettuce, Mushrooms and Peas

1 oz (25g) butter
8 large spring onions, topped and tailed, then cut into 3-inch (7.5cm) lengths
1/2 lb (225g) button mushrooms, thickly sliced
1/4 chicken stock cube
2 butterhead (soft leaf) lettuces, well rinsed and drained
1 level teaspoon sugar
1/2 lb (225g) frozen *petits pois* or ordinary peas
salt and pepper
beurre manié made with 3/4 tablespoon soft butter and 3/4 tablespoon flour

Melt the butter in a large, heavy saucepan and throw in the spring onions and mushrooms. Cook for a few minutes, until the onions are soft, then add the chicken stock cube (press it with the back of a wooden spoon into the butter to dissolve it). Shred the lettuces and add to the pan with the sugar, peas and a good seasoning of salt and pepper. Partly cover and cook for about 10–15 minutes.

Mix the butter and flour together until you have a smooth paste. Drop it, small bits at a time, into the vegetable mixture. Wait until each piece has been incorporated before you add the next, stirring carefully all the time. Check the seasoning and adjust if necessary. Serve on its own or with jacket or boiled potatoes.

Serves 2, or 3 with potatoes

10 minutes ◙ 20 minutes ✱

Stuffed Onions

4 large Spanish onions, peeled
1 oz (25g) butter
1/2 green pepper, chopped
1 lb (450g) lean minced beef or pork
1 14-oz (400g) tin Italian tomatoes
1 1/2 oz (40g) raisins
2 level tablespoons tomato purée

generous pinch of sugar
1 clove of garlic, crushed
1 tablespoon sherry
1/4 teaspoon ground cinnamon
pinch of chilli powder or ground cloves
salt and black pepper
knob of butter
8 fl oz (225ml) beef stock or water

Cut a large circle in the top of the onions (going right to the edge and digging deep) and scoop out the centres (leaving an 1/8-inch/.25 cm shell). Blanch the onion shells in boiling water for 5 minutes, or until almost soft. Lift out, invert and drain well.

Melt the butter in a heavy pan and sauté the onion centres and pepper until the onion is golden. Stir in the meat and brown quickly. Add the tomatoes, breaking them up with the side of a wooden spoon. Blend in the raisins, tomato purée, sugar, garlic, sherry and spices. Cook, stirring frequently, for about 20 minutes, until the mixture is thick but not dry. Season well with salt and pepper.

Stand the onions in a baking tin. Fill them with the meat mixture, pressing it down into the shells and piling it up slightly at the top. Add a knob of butter with the stock to the pan and put into a preheated oven (350°F/Gas Mark 4/180°C) for an hour (or until the onions are tender and lightly browned), basting frequently. Take out and serve with a crisp green salad (or simply fill the onions and bake later).

Serves 4

● 15 minutes ◘ 30 minutes + 1 hour (oven) ◖

Tomatoes with Guacamole

4 large ripe tomatoes, preferably the large salad or 'beef' variety

Guacamole
1 large ripe avocado
2 teaspoons grated onion
1/2 garlic clove, crushed (optional)
few dashes of Worcestershire sauce
1/4 teaspoon chilli powder

juice of 1/2 large ripe lemon
salt, pepper
2–3 tablespoons natural yogurt
2 rashers back bacon, cooked until crisp
chopped parsley or chervil

Wash the tomatoes and wipe dry. Carefully remove the tops and put to one side. Scoop out the innards and reserve. Turn the tomatoes upside down.

Halve the avocado and remove the stone. Scoop out the flesh, making sure you get the bright green flesh close to the skin. Put into a liquidizer or food processor with the onion, garlic, Worcestershire sauce, chilli powder, lemon juice, half the tomato innards and a good seasoning of salt and pepper. Whizz until smooth, then tip into a bowl and blend in the yogurt. Crumble the bacon into small pieces and add half to the guacamole. Check the seasoning.

Turn the tomatoes right side up and arrange on a serving dish. Fill them with the guacamole, piling it up at the top. Sprinkle with the remaining bacon bits and a little chopped parsley. Cover with cling-film if not serving immediately. Serve with a rice salad and crusty bread.

Serves 4

● 15 minutes ◒

Salads

In France, salads are not made – they are composed. Crisp leaves of radicchio, lamb's lettuce and endive are tossed judiciously in good olive oil and vinegar. Across the Channel, this simple manoeuvre runs hopelessly amok. The greenery is caught lounging in the bottom of a bowl – anaesthetized by too much oil. The odd slice of cucumber or tomato sprawls uncomfortably on top. The sight of a *good* salad is so unexpected that it stops the conversation as quickly as a well-risen soufflé.

We used to have a wonderful excuse for this failing: everything was too expensive or out of season. But now greengrocers and supermarkets are breaking their necks to find tempting saladstuffs. In one supermarket in *mid-February*, I counted twenty-four fresh salad ingredients. Under the same roof, there were ten sorts of mustard, seven oils and five different vinegars. The permutations of these would provide a different salad every night for a month.

If salad is to be a meal, then it is worth making it interesting. A curly endive may be four times as expensive as a butterhead lettuce – but it keeps well and goes four times as far. Dressed with hot oil, bacon bits and croûtons, it becomes the stylish *salade frisée aux lardons*. Iceberg lettuce is equally good value, providing a good foil for chicken, ham and cheese. Use a glut of apples to delicious advantage – combine them with leftover turkey or chicken, toasted walnuts, raisins, celery and homemade mayonnaise.

A warm salad is not as incongruous as it sounds. Chicken livers, browned quickly so that they're still pink inside, are tossed with crisp spinach leaves, olive oil and vinegar. Pasta shells and bows can be taken straight from the pot and mixed in a mustardy mayonnaise with red pepper, broccoli, ham and beans.

If salad ingredients are limited, improvise. Tinned sweetcorn mixed with spring onions and vinaigrette is a good partner for cold meat; grated carrots could be mixed with apples, peanuts and raisins; frozen beans can be cooked briefly, then tossed in a hot bacon dressing. For crunch, add croûtons, chopped fennel, apple or toasted nuts. To give a contrasting taste – add diced avocado, dates, cheese, hard-boiled egg or anchovies.

Good olive oil does, unquestionably, produce a more distinctive salad dressing. To stretch it further, make the vinaigrette with 2 parts olive oil and 1 part corn or peanut oil. Different vinegars can subtly change the character of a dressing and are easily made at home: put a few sprigs of a fresh herb (tarragon, basil, rosemary, thyme – any one of these) or several cloves of garlic into a bottle of white wine vinegar, close tightly and leave for at least six weeks.

23

New Potato and Frankfurter Salad

Children who normally baulk at salads seem to find this one irresistible.

1 lb (450g) new potatoes
2 extra-long frankfurters
   (6 oz/175g total weight)

4 oz (100g) celery, chopped

Dressing

1 rounded teaspoon Dijon or
   German mustard
1 tablespoon white wine
   vinegar
4 tablespoons good olive oil

1 tablespoon finely chopped
   spring onion tops or chives
salt and black pepper
1 tablespoon finely chopped
   fresh parsley

Scrub the potatoes and cook in their skins until just tender. Drain well then cut, while still warm, into thick slices (or if small, simply halve them). While the potatoes cook, heat the frankfurters very gently in a saucepan of water (the water should never boil – just barely 'shuddering'). Then take out, drain well and cut into diagonal chunks. Put in a serving dish with the potatoes and chopped celery.

Measure the mustard and vinegar into a small bowl and whisk in the oil until you have a thickish vinaigrette. Blend in the spring onions and season to taste with salt and black pepper. Pour over the warm salad and toss carefully. Scatter chopped parsley over the top and serve warm or cool.

Serves 2–3

🍴 15 minutes   🍲 15 minutes   🥣 (but don't refrigerate) ✸

24

Italian Salad with Tuna and Peppers

6 oz (175g) pasta shells
10 oz (275g) peas
1 small red pepper, chopped
2 spring onions, chopped
2 large stalks celery, chopped

1 7-oz (200g) tin tuna, well
   drained of oil
6 ripe tomatoes, washed and
   dried
chopped parsley or chives to
   garnish

Dressing

2 level teaspoons French
   mustard
pinch of sugar
2 tablespoons white wine
   vinegar

6 tablespoons olive or
   vegetable oil
6 tablespoons mayonnaise
salt and pepper

Cook the pasta in plenty of boiling, salted water until *al dente*. Drain well and put to one side. Cook the peas briefly (a minute or so, no longer) and refresh under cold water. Leave to drain.

Measure the mustard, sugar and vinegar into a large mixing bowl. Blend together well, then slowly whisk in the oil. Mix in the mayonnaise and season well.

Add the pasta, peas, pepper, onions and celery and turn carefully with a wooden spoon until well coated with the dressing. Pat the tuna dry with kitchen paper and break into chunks. Cut the tomatoes into quarters or eighths (depending on their size). Add these to the salad, season again with salt and pepper and toss carefully. Scatter a little chopped parsley or chives over the top and serve (or cover with cling-film and leave until needed).

Serves 6

🍴 25 minutes   🍲 5 minutes   🥣

Chicken Salad with Brazil Nuts and Grapes

4 large, cooked chicken breasts
2 large stalks celery
4 oz (100g) brazil nuts

$^1/_2$ lb (225g) black or green grapes or a mixture of the two

Dressing

1 teaspoon French mustard
1 spring onion, finely chopped
1 tablespoon tarragon vinegar
salt and pepper
3 tablespoons olive or vegetable oil

4 tablespoons mayonnaise
2 tablespoons finely chopped parsley
salt and pepper

Remove the skin and bone from the chicken breasts, then cut into bite-size chunks. Wash the celery and dry well in kitchen paper. Chop into medium dice and put into a large mixing bowl with the chicken and brazil nuts. Wash and dry the grapes well, then halve and remove the pips. Add to the bowl with the other ingredients.

Mix the mustard, spring onion, vinegar and a little salt and pepper together in a small bowl. Whisk in the oil slowly, then blend in the mayonnaise and 1 tablespoon of parsley. Taste and adjust the seasoning if necessary. Pour over the salad and toss carefully until thoroughly blended. Scatter the remaining parsley over the top. Transfer to a glass bowl and serve with new potatoes (or fluffy white rice) and a plain lettuce salad.

Serves 4

◖ 15–20 minutes ◑

Turkey Waldorf

$^1/_2$ lb (225g) cooked turkey meat (boned)
salt and pepper
6 tablespoons mayonnaise
3–4 tablespoons single cream
good squeeze of lemon juice

2 oz (50g) walnuts, roughly chopped
2 large celery stalks, diced
2 oz (50g) raisins
3 crisp red apples
chopped chervil or parsley

Cut the turkey into bite-size pieces and season lightly with salt and pepper.

Measure the mayonnaise into a large mixing bowl and add enough cream to give it the consistency of double cream. Season to taste with lemon juice, salt and pepper. Add the walnuts, celery and raisins. Peel, core and chop the apples, then add to the bowl with the turkey chunks. Carefully toss the mixture until well coated with the dressing. Taste and adjust the seasoning if necessary. Transfer to a serving dish and give a light dusting of chopped chervil or parsley. Serve with a crisp lettuce or green bean salad.

Serves 4

◖ 20 minutes ◑

Salade Niçoise

2 heads Cos lettuce or 1 large Webb's Wonder or 1 iceberg lettuce
4 ripe tomatoes, washed and quartered
4 oz (100g) green beans, cooked but still crisp

3 large hard-boiled eggs
8–10 black olives
1 2-oz (50g) tin anchovy fillets
1 7-oz (200g) tin tuna, well drained of oil
salt and pepper

Dressing

1 teaspoon French mustard
2 tablespoons white wine vinegar
salt and pepper

6 tablespoons olive or vegetable oil
chopped herbs

Wash and dry the lettuce well. Tear into manageable pieces and put into a salad bowl. Arrange the tomatoes, rounded side up, round the edge of the bowl, then a row of beans just inside them. Cut the eggs into quarters and arrange pinwheel fashion from the centre, leaving room in the middle. Put the olives and anchovies between the eggs. Break the tuna into bite-size chunks and pile up in the middle. Season lightly with salt and pepper.

Mix the mustard and vinegar with a little salt and pepper in a small bowl. Whisk in the oil slowly and blend in any fresh herbs you can lay your hands on. Taste and adjust the seasoning if necessary. Pour over the salad and toss it when at the table (or cover the bowl with cling-film and add the dressing just before serving).

Serves 4–6

 20 minutes 5 minutes

26

English Apple, Date and Asparagus Salad

6 oz (175g) dates, fresh if possible
4 crisp English apples, preferably green-skinned

1 12-oz (350g) tin green asparagus spears or pieces, drained of juice
4 oz (100g) good Cheddar, diced

Dressing

1 teaspoon French mustard
good pinch of sugar
salt and pepper
1 tablespoon lemon juice
1 tablespoon white wine vinegar

6 tablespoons olive or vegetable oil
chopped chervil or parsley

Wash and dry the dates, then halve and remove the stones. Cut into thin, lengthwise strips. Wash and dry the apples, then quarter, core and cut into medium chunks.

Mix the mustard, sugar, good seasoning of salt and pepper, lemon juice and vinegar in a large mixing bowl. Gradually whisk in the oil with a little chopped chervil or parsley. Taste and adjust the seasoning if necessary. Add the dates, apple and cheese and toss well.

Transfer the salad to a large bowl or platter and arrange the asparagus on top. Scatter a little chervil or parsley on top and serve (or cover with cling-film and leave for 1–2 hours – but no longer, otherwise the asparagus will predominate and the apples discolour).

Serves 6

 20 minutes

New Potato, Ham and Celery Salad

1¹/₂ lbs (675g) new potatoes
5 large stalks celery, cut into thick chunks
2 tablespoons white wine vinegar
salt and pepper

¹/₄ pint (150ml) double cream
juice of ¹/₂ small lemon
4 oz (100g) cooked ham, cut in thin strips
chopped parsley and celery leaves to finish

Scrub the potatoes, then cook in lightly salted water until just tender. Drain well and when cool enough to handle, cut into thick slices. Put them in a large mixing bowl with the celery and pour over the vinegar. Season well with salt and pepper and toss carefully. Allow to cool completely (but don't refrigerate).

Whisk the cream until thick, then blend in the lemon juice and a little salt and pepper. Pour over the potatoes and mix carefully. Add the ham, then transfer it all to a serving dish. Toss again carefully, then scatter a little chopped parsley on top and put a row of celery leaves down the middle. Cover with cling-film and leave until needed (this can even be made the day before). Serve with brown rolls and something very green (perhaps broccoli, beans or peas).

Serves 4

 20 minutes ◧ 15 minutes ◐

Tomato and Mozzarella Salad with Basil

2 large 'beef' or salad tomatoes *or* 4 small
1 7-oz (200g) fresh Mozzarella cheese

1 2-oz (50g) tin anchovy fillets, well drained
a few black olives
salt and black pepper

Dressing
1 tablespoon white wine vinegar
¹/₂ teaspoon French mustard
salt and pepper

3–4 tablespoons good olive oil
1 tablespoon fresh basil, finely chopped, or ¹/₂ tablespoon dried

Wash and dry the tomatoes and cut into thin crosswise slices. Cut the Mozzarella into similarly thin slices. Take two large plates and arrange half the tomato slices on each one. Slip the cheese slices in between the tomatoes, then arrange the anchovy fillets (if they're very salty, soak them for a few minutes in milk, then pat dry with kitchen paper) in a lattice pattern on top of each salad. Halve the olives and use them to fill the spaces left by the anchovies. Season well with salt and black pepper.

Mix the vinegar, mustard and salt together in a small bowl. Gradually whisk in the oil, then add a little pepper and more salt if needed. Blend in half the basil and pour over the tomatoes and cheese. Scatter the remaining basil on top. Serve with lots of warm crusty French bread and unsalted butter.

Serves 2

 15 minutes ✳

27

Spinach Salad with Mushrooms and Bacon

The hallmark of every chic Manhattan restaurant, this salad occasionally comes dressed with diced avocado, walnuts or hard-boiled egg.

1 lb (450g) fresh young spinach	4 oz (100g) button mushrooms
4 rashers back bacon	handful of wholemeal croûtons
	salt and black pepper

Mustard Vinaigrette

2 rounded teaspoons pale French mustard	2 tablespoons white wine vinegar
good pinch of sugar	6–8 tablespoons olive oil
	salt and pepper

Remove the stalks from the spinach and any leaves that are soggy or bruised. Soak the good leaves in a basin of cold water for at least 20 minutes, then lift out, drain and dry well. Grill the bacon until crisp, then cut into julienne strips. Wipe the mushrooms and slice thinly. Put the bacon and croûtons on a plate and into a warm oven.

Put the mustard with the sugar into a small bowl. Add the vinegar, a little salt and mix together well. Then whisk in the oil gradually, until you have a thick, creamy vinaigrette. Season with pepper and a little more salt if needed.

Pull the spinach into medium-sized pieces and place in a large salad bowl. Scatter the mushrooms, bacon strips and croûtons on top. Season lightly with salt and pepper, then pour on half the dressing and toss until every leaf is glistening. Add more if you need it, then serve.

Serves 4–6

◗ 20 minutes   ◉ 5 minutes

28

Spinach, Avocado and Apple Salad

2 large slices white bread, crusts removed	1/2 lb (225g) spinach, washed and dried, stalks removed
a little butter	1 large ripe avocado
1/2 clove of garlic	2 large, crisp, red apples

Creamy Vinaigrette

1 egg yolk	4–5 tablespoons olive oil
1 teaspoon pale French mustard	salt and pepper
1 1/2 tablespoons white wine vinegar	

Butter both sides of the bread and rub with garlic. Cut into small dice, transfer to a baking sheet in a hot oven and leave until the croûtons are crisp and golden. Keep warm until needed.

Mix the yolk, mustard and a little salt in a small bowl. Add the vinegar, then whisk in the oil gradually. Season with pepper and more salt if needed.

Tear the spinach into manageable pieces. Place in a large salad bowl. Halve the avocado, remove the stone, scoop out the flesh and cut into medium chunks. Wash and dry the apples, then quarter and core. Chop into chunks roughly the same size as the avocado. Scatter the avocado and apple over the spinach. Rescue the croûtons from the oven and sprinkle on top. Whisk the dressing and pour over most of it (you may not need it all and too much would spoil the salad's crispness). Toss and serve.

Serves 4

◗ 20 minutes   ◉ 20 minutes

Winter Cabbage Salad

4 oz (100g) dried apricots or dried peaches or a mixture of both
4 oz (100g) seedless raisins
5 tablespoons orange juice
1/2 small white cabbage

2 oz (50g) toasted hazelnuts, halved
5 oz (150g) fresh dates, quartered and stoned
2 small oranges, peeled and sliced lengthwise
chopped parsley or chervil

Dressing
1 egg yolk
1 teaspoon French mustard
1/2 teaspoon sugar
1 tablespoon white wine vinegar

6 tablespoons olive or vegetable oil
salt and pepper

Coarsely chop the apricots and put into a medium bowl with the raisins. Pour over the orange juice and leave to marinate for at least an hour (basting with the juice occasionally).

Finely shred the cabbage, rinse under cold water and dry completely. Transfer to a large salad bowl, then add the nuts and dates.

Mix the egg yolk, mustard, sugar and vinegar together in a small bowl or the bowl of a food processor. Whisk in (or blend electrically) the oil slowly, until you have a thickish, very creamy dressing. Whisk in the juices from the dried fruit and season to taste with salt and pepper. Use enough of the dressing to coat the cabbage (don't overdo this or it will become soggy), then blend in the apricots, raisins and sliced oranges. Toss lightly, then dust with chopped parsley.

Serves 8

🥄 20 minutes   Soaking time: 1 hour   ⬤

Californian Coleslaw

1/2 small white cabbage
2 large carrots, peeled
1 crisp apple, quartered and cored

3 courgettes, topped and tailed
1 small onion, peeled and very finely sliced
handful of Californian raisins

Dressing
1 generous teaspoon French mustard
1 tablespoon white wine vinegar
salt

3 tablespoons olive or vegetable oil
1/4 pint (150ml) soured cream
pepper
chopped dill or parsley

Shred the cabbage finely and rinse well under cold running water. Drain and dry well. Cut the carrots, apple and courgettes into long, very thin julienne strips. (You can grate them in a food processor – but this tends to make them a bit mushy.) Put them all into a large salad bowl with the cabbage, onion and raisins.

Mix the mustard, vinegar and salt together in a small bowl. Gradually whisk in the oil, then the soured cream. Season with pepper and more salt if needed. Pour over the salad and toss carefully. Taste and adjust the seasoning if necessary. Scatter a little chopped dill or parsley over the top and leave for 1–2 hours before serving (toss again before taking to the table).

Serves 8

🥄 20 minutes

29

Frizzy Salad with Bacon

The bitterness of the curly endive is combatted here by the sweet flavour of bacon and walnuts.

1/2 curly endive (failing that, Batavian endive)
1 bunch of watercress
5 tablespoons walnut or olive oil *or* half and half
3 oz (75g) streaky bacon, finely chopped

2 oz (50g) shelled walnuts
2 tablespoons white wine vinegar
good pinch of sugar
salt and pepper

Rinse the endive well under cold running water, drain well and dry in a tea towel. Do the same with the watercress. Remove the root end of the endive and separate the leaves. Place in a salad bowl and put the watercress, roughly shredded, on top.

Put 3 tablespoons of oil into a medium saucepan. Add the bacon and walnuts and cook until the bacon is crisp. Add the remaining oil to the pan and, when really hot, pour over the salad. Put the vinegar and sugar in the same pan, stir until the sugar has dissolved and, when hot, tip over the salad. Season with salt and pepper, toss quickly and serve.

Serves 4

 10 minutes ◉ 10 minutes ✳

Carrot Salad with Nuts and Raisins

1 lb (450g) carrots, peeled and roughly chopped
2 spring onions, topped and tailed

Dressing
1 1/2 teaspoons pale French mustard
good pinch of brown sugar
salt
1 1/2 tablespoons white wine vinegar

1 bunch of watercress, shredded
2 oz (50g) seedless raisins
2 oz (50g) salted peanuts

4–5 tablespoons olive or vegetable oil
pepper

Put the carrots into a food processor and blend until finely chopped (or use a hand-chopper or grater – but this is hard work). Tip into a salad bowl, then add the spring onions, finely chopped, with the watercress, raisins and peanuts.

Mix the mustard, sugar and salt together in a small bowl. Blend in the vinegar, then gradually whisk in the oil. Season with pepper and more salt if needed. Pour enough of the dressing on the carrots to coat them lightly. Toss and taste for seasoning. Add a little more dressing if necessary, then cover and leave for at least half an hour before serving.

Serves 4

 20 minutes ◓

Tabbouleh

A variation of the classic Middle Eastern salad – light and refreshing, ideal for summer suppers. The bulgur can be found in any health shop and most delicatessens.

1/2 lb (225g) bulgur (cracked wheat)
6 good-sized spring onions, chopped
3 tablespoons chopped fresh mint (halve quantity if using dried)
3 tablespoons chopped fresh parsley
1/2 large cucumber, diced
1 tablespoon toasted sunflower seeds (optional)
salt and black pepper
3 tablespoons lemon juice
5 tablespoons good olive oil
2 oz (50g) toasted hazelnuts

Put the bulgur in a large bowl, cover with cold water and leave to soak for at least 30 minutes. Drain in a sieve then lift out with a slotted spoon and spread out on a clean tea towel or double thickness of kitchen paper. Leave for 1 1/2–2 hours to dry.

Put the bulgur in a large mixing bowl. Mix in the spring onions, mint, parsley, cucumber and seeds. Add a good seasoning of salt and pepper. Mix the lemon juice and oil together (as for a vinaigrette) in a small bowl, then pour over the bulgur. Mix well, then blend in the hazelnuts and check the seasoning. Cover and leave for several hours so the flavour can mature. Delicious served with cold lamb or beef.

Serves 6

➥ 20 minutes   Soaking/drying time: about 2 hours   ◀

Brown Rice Salad with Watercress and Peanuts

6 oz (175g) brown rice
1/4 teaspoon salt
1 spring onion, finely chopped
2 oz (50g) green peas, cooked
2 oz (50g) seedless raisins
2 oz (50g) dry roasted peanuts
1/2 medium green pepper, chopped (optional)
1/2 bunch of watercress, shredded

Dressing
1 teaspoon French mustard
1 tablespoon wine vinegar
salt
3–4 tablespoons olive or vegetable oil
pepper
2 tablespoons finely chopped fresh parsley

Put the rice with 1/4 teaspoon salt and double its volume in water into a large saucepan. Cover and simmer gently for about 45 minutes or until all the water has been absorbed. Shake the pan to prevent sticking, then leave covered for 5–10 minutes, off the heat. Allow to cool completely, then fork through carefully to separate the grains and tip into a salad bowl. Add the peas, raisins, peanuts, green pepper (if used) and shredded watercress.

Mix the mustard, vinegar and a little salt together in a small bowl. Whisk in the oil slowly to make a creamy vinaigrette. Season to taste with pepper and more salt if needed. Add to the salad with the parsley and toss carefully until thoroughly blended. Very good with cold ham or simple egg dishes.

Serves 4–6

➥ 10 minutes   ▣ 45 minutes

See page 122 for alternative salad dressings

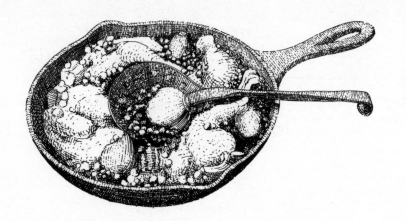

Chicken and Turkey

The price we pay for cheap chicken is a bird of nondescript character. Intensive breeding has produced uniform quality and size but remarkably little flavour. Unless you have a ready source of free-range chickens, the battery variety is the one most likely to turn up on your table.

Roasting can be the best and the most boring way of cooking chicken. It is no longer enough to pop it in the oven and hope for the best. For maximum flavour and crispness, rub the bird all over with a generous amount of butter, put a few sprigs of fresh tarragon or an apple in the neck cavity and place in a tin with several cups of chicken stock or white wine. Baste it religiously, turning the bird on one side then the other so that it browns evenly. A simple gravy can be made by adding vegetable stock, wine or water to the pan juices.

Diehards who insist on chipolatas and bread sauce with their chicken might be pleasantly surprised by a hotter European sausage or tart gooseberry jelly instead. An unusual stuffing – perhaps pistachio nuts, apricots and breadcrumbs – would perk up any bird.

A chicken brick (not a brick at all, but a large egg-shape of terracotta which fits together neatly) produces a bird so juicy that the meat literally falls from the bone. Provided sea salt and plenty of fresh herbs are cooked with it, the flavour is excellent.

When chicken is to be subjected to intense heat (when grilling or barbecuing), it's advisable to marinate it first. The marinade may be a simple mixture of oil, lemon juice or herbs, discarded before cooking, or a spicier sauce which is also used to baste the chicken as it cooks (this must be done with care because the sauce will burn if placed too close to the heat). If using chicken breasts, flatten them first with a rolling pin to ensure that they grill evenly.

The aromas wafting from any Indian restaurant are proof enough of the affinity of chicken with spices. Even without a Tandoori oven and freshly ground spices, it's still possible to produce a fairly good imitation at home. Ready-ground spices, if properly stored and not kept too long, provide an acceptable substitute. Ground cumin, coriander, cardamom, turmeric, ginger, cinnamon, allspice, cloves – any of these would suit a chicken. Marinate the bird (or chicken pieces) in a blend of yogurt, spices, lemon juice and a little garlic for a few hours or overnight. Then bake or grill, whenever you feel like eating it.

The Shoemaker's Chicken

1 oz (25g) butter
6 oz (175g) *chorizo* (sweet Spanish) or spicy pork sausages
1 medium onion, peeled and finely sliced
2 large stalks celery, chopped
1/2 pint (275ml) chicken stock

1 lb (450g) ripe tomatoes, roughly chopped
4 large chicken breasts, boned and skin removed
salt and pepper
2 tablespoons finely chopped parsley

Melt the butter in a large, flameproof casserole. Prick the sausages all over with a fork and brown in the butter for 5–10 minutes. Lift out and put to one side. Add the onion to the pan with the celery and cook slowly until the onion is golden. Pour in the chicken stock, scraping the bottom of the pan to loosen the sediment. Add the tomatoes to the pan with the sausage, chopped diagonally into 1-inch (2.5cm) chunks. Cut the chicken into large chunks and add to the pan with a good seasoning of salt and pepper and half the chopped parsley. Bring up to the boil, then cover and put into a preheated oven (350°F/Gas Mark 4/180°C) for an hour, or until the chicken is tender. Skim off any fat from the top, check the seasoning and dust lightly with the remaining parsley. Serve with fluffy white rice and a green salad.

Serves 4

 15 minutes   ◙ 20 minutes + 1 hour (oven)   ◕

Chicken with Leeks and Bacon

1 oz (25g) butter
4 chicken breasts
1 small onion, peeled and sliced
3 rashers unsmoked back bacon, cut into thin strips
4 large leeks, well rinsed and cut into 1-inch (2.5cm) chunks

3/4 pint (425ml) chicken stock
1 large egg yolk
1/4 pint (150ml) double cream
salt and pepper
squeeze of lemon juice
chopped chervil or parsley

Melt the butter in a large, heavy casserole. Brown the chicken quickly on all sides (do this in batches rather than crowd the pan). Lift out and put to one side. Add the onion and bacon to the pan and cook until the onion is golden, the bacon crisp. Add the leeks and stir until well coated with the buttery juices. Cover the pot and 'sweat' for 5 minutes. Uncover, pour in the stock and bring up to the boil. Add the chicken, cover and reduce the heat. Simmer gently for 40 minutes or until the chicken is tender.*

Lift the chicken out of the casserole (reheated gently if prepared ahead) with a slotted spoon and arrange on a heated serving dish. Put the leeks and bacon round the chicken and keep warm. Skim off excess fat, then boil the liquid in the casserole rapidly until reduced by half. Mix the egg yolk and cream together, then pour it all into the pan. Season with salt, pepper and a squeeze of lemon juice. Whisk over gentle heat until steaming and slightly thickened. Pour over the chicken and leeks, give a light dusting with chervil or parsley and take to the table. Serve with new potatoes and perhaps a few crisp green beans.

Serves 4

 10 minutes   ◙ about 1 hour   ◕ to *

Poulet Grand'mère

¹/₂ oz (15g) butter	¹/₄ pint (150ml) dry white
1 tablespoon vegetable oil	wine
4 large chicken breasts	¹/₂ lb (225g) small new
4 oz (100g) button	potatoes, well scrubbed
mushrooms, thickly sliced	2 tablespoons finely chopped
3 oz (75g) unsmoked back	parsley or chervil
bacon, diced	salt and pepper
³/₄ pint (425ml) chicken stock	1 oz (25g) butter to finish

Heat the butter and oil in a large sauté pan with a lid (or flameproof casserole). When hot, add the chicken breasts and brown well on both sides. Lift out with a slotted spoon and put to one side. Add the mushrooms to the same pan and cook quickly until just softened. Lift out and keep warm with the chicken.

Cook the bacon dice in the sauté pan until almost crisp. Pour in the stock and wine, scraping the bottom of the pan well to loosen the sediment. Return the chicken to the pan with the potatoes and 1 tablespoon of parsley. Bring up to the boil, then cover and reduce the heat. Simmer gently for 30–40 minutes or until the chicken is tender. Add the mushrooms and their juices for the last 5 minutes of cooking time.*

Lift the chicken pieces out of the pan (having reheated it gently if prepared ahead) and place in a hot serving dish. With a slotted spoon, scoop out the potatoes, mushrooms and bacon and arrange round the chicken. Skim off any fat, then season the pan juices with a little salt and black pepper. Gradually whisk in the butter (over a very low heat). Pour it over the chicken, dust with parsley and serve.

Serves 4

◖ 10 minutes   ◙ 55 minutes   ◗ to *

34

Chicken with Marmalade Marinade

4 large chicken breasts

Marinade

1 oz (25g) butter	juice and grated rind of 1 ripe
2 level tablespoons light	lemon
brown sugar	2 tablespoons dry sherry
3 level teaspoons pale French	6 tablespoons orange
mustard	marmalade

Put all the marinade ingredients into a small saucepan and stir over a low heat until well blended. Bring to the boil, then simmer gently for about 3 minutes. Take off the heat and put to one side to cool slightly.

Wipe the chicken breasts with kitchen paper, then flatten them with a rolling pin. Line a shallow tin with foil and arrange the breasts on it. Season with salt and pepper, then coat them with two-thirds of the marinade. Leave in a cool place for several hours.*

When ready to cook, heat the oven to 375°F/Gas Mark 5/190°C. Bake the chicken on the second shelf from the top of the oven for 40–45 minutes, basting occasionally with the pan juices. Then take out, brush with the remaining marinade and put under a hot grill (about 3 inches/7.5cm from it) until the skin is crisp and nicely browned (watch carefully as it burns easily).

Serves 4

◖ 10 minutes   Marinating time: several hours or overnight
◙ about 50 minutes   ◗ to *

Baked Chicken Maryland

4 large chicken breasts
1^1/$_2$ oz (40g) flour
salt and black pepper
1 egg, lightly beaten
10 tablespoons dried white
   breadcrumbs
1 tablespoon chopped fresh
   tarragon (halve the quantity
   if using dried)

1 tablespoon finely chopped
   parsley
2^1/$_2$ oz (65g) butter
1 tablespoon vegetable oil

Wipe the chicken breasts with kitchen paper and flatten with a rolling pin. Mix the flour with a good seasoning of salt and pepper on a large plate. Toss the chicken breasts well in it, shaking off any excess. Dip each piece first in the beaten egg, then roll in the breadcrumbs which have been mixed with the chopped tarragon and parsley. Season the chicken lightly with salt and pepper.

Melt the butter with the oil in a large, shallow baking tin and arrange the chicken in it. Baste well with the butter, then place in a preheated oven (400°F/Gas Mark 6/200°C) on the second shelf from the top. Bake for 45–55 minutes or until the chicken is crisp, brown and tender. Take out and serve with sweetcorn and bananas which have been lightly sautéed in butter (or serve the chicken cold).

Serves 4

◖ 15 minutes   ◉ 50 minutes   ◑ ▲▲ ✳

Honeyed Chicken with Meaux Mustard

3 tablespoons Meaux mustard
1^1/$_2$ tablespoons soft brown
   sugar
2 tablespoons thick honey
^{1}/$_2$ oz (15g) butter

6 plump chicken thighs
salt and pepper
2 tablespoons orange juice
1 tablespoon medium dry
   sherry

Preheat the oven to 375°F/Gas Mark 5/190°C. Put the mustard into a small bowl and gradually blend in the sugar and honey to make a smooth, creamy mixture.

Melt the butter in a small, shallow roasting tin, then place the chicken in it. Season well with salt and pepper, then coat them with two-thirds of the mustard mixture. Bake near the top of the oven for 20 minutes, basting occasionally with the pan juices. Then coat with the remaining mustard sauce and return to the oven for a further 20 minutes.

Line a grill pan (or baking tin) with foil and arrange the chicken in it. Put under a moderate grill (about 3 inches/8.5cm from it) to crisp the skin (watch it carefully). At the same time, place the roasting tin with the pan juices over moderate heat. Skim off the fat, then add the orange juice and sherry. Stir until well blended, then simmer for 3–4 minutes until slightly syrupy. Transfer the chicken to individual plates, coat with the hot sauce and serve at once with watercress and fluffy white rice.

Serves 2–3

◖ 5 minutes   ◉ 5 minutes + 40 minutes (oven)   ✳

35

Chinese Chicken with Nuts and Celery

Don't be dismayed by the length of the ingredients: once you've done the chopping, the rest is easy.

4 large chicken breasts, boned with skin removed
3 tablespoons vegetable oil
8 spring onions, topped, tailed and cut into 2-inch (5cm) lengths
3 large stalks celery, cut into 1/2-inch (1cm) chunks

1 large green pepper, cut into thin strips
1 clove of garlic, crushed
1 5-oz (150g) tin water chestnuts, drained (optional)
4 oz (100g) dry roasted peanuts or cashews
salt and pepper

Sauce
1 level tablespoon cornflour
1/4 teaspoon ground ginger
1 tablespoon vegetable oil
3 tablespoons soy sauce
3 tablespoons water

2 1/2 tablespoons granulated sugar
1 tablespoon white wine vinegar
3 fl oz (75ml) dry sherry

Start by making the sauce. Blend the cornflour and the ginger together in a small bowl. Gradually blend in the oil, soy sauce, water, sugar, vinegar and sherry.

Cut the chicken into bite-size chunks. Heat the oil in your largest, heaviest sauté pan. When very hot, add the chicken pieces, onions, celery, green pepper, crushed garlic and water chestnuts (if used). Stir-fry for about 5 minutes or until the chicken is cooked through. Pour in the sauce with the peanuts and stir for about a minute until slightly thickened and hot. Take off the heat, season to taste with salt and pepper and serve with hot, fluffy white rice.

Serves 4

🍴 20 minutes   ▣ 10 minutes   ◑   ✳

36

Chicken with Broccoli, Beans and Red Pepper

1/2 oz (15g) butter
1 tablespoon vegetable oil
8 spring onions, topped, tailed and cut in half
1 small red pepper, sliced thinly
2 chicken breasts, skinned and boned
1/4 pint (150ml) chicken stock or dry white wine (or half and half)

1/2 lb (225g) calabrese or broccoli, separated into florets
1/2 lb (225g) French beans
good squeeze of lemon juice
salt and black pepper

Heat the butter and oil in a large, heavy sauté pan. Cook the spring onions and pepper until the onions are soft. Cut the chicken into bite-size pieces and add to the pan. Stir-fry until it turns white. Add half the chicken stock or white wine, broccoli and beans. Partly cover and cook rapidly for 5 minutes, shaking the pan occasionally. Add the remaining stock, partly cover and cook for a further 5 minutes. Then add a good squeeze of lemon juice and season well with salt and freshly ground black pepper. Serve with rice or jacket potatoes.

Serves 2

🍴 15 minutes   ▣ 15 minutes   ✳

Quick Tandoori Chicken

4 large chicken breasts *or* 8 smaller chicken pieces

$1^{1}/_{2}$ level tablespoons Sharwood's tandoori mixture

$1/_{2}$ pint (275ml) natural yogurt

2 tablespoons fresh lime or lemon juice

1 dessertspoon peeled and grated fresh ginger *or* 1 level teaspoon ground ginger

salt and pepper

Remove the skin from the chicken and cut several diagonal slashes in the flesh. Mix the tandoori mixture with the yogurt, lime juice, ginger and a good seasoning of salt and pepper.

Line a shallow baking tin with foil and arrange the chicken pieces on it. Coat with the marinade mixture, then cover the tin with foil. Leave in a cool place for several hours or overnight.

When ready to cook, remove the foil and bake the chicken in a hot oven (400°F/Gas Mark 6/200°C) for 30 minutes. Then put under a hot grill for about 5 minutes. Serve with plain or spiced rice and a green salad.

Serves 4

🥄 10 minutes   Marinating time: several hours or overnight
🍲 35 minutes   ◀

Spiced Chicken

$1^{1}/_{2}$ oz (40g) butter

1 medium onion, peeled and finely chopped

1 clove of garlic, crushed

1 level tablespoon peeled and chopped fresh ginger *or* $1^{1}/_{2}$ level teaspoons ground ginger

2 level tablespoons mild curry powder

$1/_{2}$ teaspoon mixed spice

$3/_{4}$ pint (425ml) chicken stock

5 tablespoons mango chutney

2 tablespoons brown sugar

1 $3^{1}/_{2}$-lb (1.5 kilos) chicken

1 level teaspoon garam masala (optional)

juice of 1 small lemon

salt and pepper

4 large bananas

Melt the butter in a medium saucepan and sauté the onion until soft and transparent. Stir in the garlic, ginger, curry powder and mixed spice and cook gently for a few minutes. Gradually add the stock and bring to a simmer. Blend in the mango chutney and brown sugar.

Wipe the chicken with kitchen paper then place in a large casserole with tight-fitting lid. Pour over the curry mixture. Cover and put into a preheated oven (325°F/Gas Mark 3/170°C) for 2 hours. Remove the lid after $1^{1}/_{2}$ hours to allow the chicken to brown and the liquid to reduce. At the same time, mix in the garam masala (if used) and the lemon juice.* (If you're in a hurry to eat, cook the chicken at 350°F/Gas Mark 4/180°C for $1^{1}/_{2}$ hours.)

Lift the chicken out of the casserole (having reheated it gently if prepared ahead). Carve and arrange the pieces in a serving dish. Skim the fat off the liquid in the casserole. Taste and correct the seasoning as needed. Pour the sauce over the chicken and serve with sliced bananas, fluffy white or spiced rice and additional chutney.

Serves 4

🥄 10 minutes   🍲 5 minutes + 2 hours (oven)   ◀ to *

Butter Roast Chicken

1 tablespoon finely chopped
  fresh or dried tarragon
2 oz (50g) soft butter
1 3^1/$_2$-lb (1.5 kilos) chicken
salt and black pepper
juice of ^{1}/$_2$ lemon

^{3}/$_4$ pint (425ml) weak chicken
  stock
beurre manié made with ^{1}/$_2$
  tablespoon butter mixed
  with ^{1}/$_2$ tablespoon flour

Preheat the oven to 400°F/Gas Mark 6/200°C. Mash the butter with the tarragon and a good seasoning of salt and pepper. Put a good knob of this inside the chicken, then rub the remainder all over the skin. Season the bird well with salt and pepper, then place in a shallow roasting tin. Squeeze the lemon juice over the chicken, then pour half the stock into the tin. Cover the chicken with a buttered paper and put into the oven. After 20 minutes, turn the bird on its side and baste with the pan juices. After another 20 minutes, turn to its other side and baste again, adding the remaining stock at the same time. When the next 20 minutes are up, stand the bird upright again, baste and continue to cook until tender (15–20 minutes). (Test by pushing a skewer through the thigh – if clear juices run out, it's done.)

Transfer the chicken to a heated serving platter and keep warm. Put the roasting tin over a low heat on the stove. Skim off excess fat, then add ^{1}/$_4$ pint (150ml) water. Simmer gently until well blended, then whisk in the *beurre manié*, small bits at a time, until the sauce has thickened slightly. Taste and adjust the seasoning if necessary, then serve.

Serves 4

▼ 10 minutes   ◉ 10 minutes + 1^1/$_4$ hours (oven)

Chicken in a Pot

2 tablespoons vegetable oil
1 3^1/$_2$-lb (1.5 kilos) chicken
1 oz (25g) butter
1 medium onion, peeled and
  sliced
salt and pepper
2 large carrots, peeled and cut
  into thin strips

2 large leeks, washed and cut
  into 1-inch (2.5cm) chunks
^{1}/$_2$ small swede, peeled and
  cut into medium chunks
^{3}/$_4$ pint (425ml) chicken stock
^{1}/$_4$ pint (150ml) single cream
2 large egg yolks
1^1/$_2$ tablespoons finely
  chopped parsley or chervil

Heat the oil in a large, flameproof casserole. Brown the chicken quickly on all sides, then lift out. Tip the oil out of the casserole.

Melt the butter in the same pan and add the onion. Cook over moderate heat until golden. Push to one side of the casserole and put the chicken back in. Cover with the onions and season well with salt and pepper. Roast, covered, in a preheated oven (400°F/Gas Mark 6/200°C) for half an hour.

Take the pot out of the oven and pour in the chicken stock. Tip in all the vegetables and pile round the chicken. Cover and return to the oven for 30 minutes longer. Then lift the chicken out and place in a serving dish, surrounded by all the vegetables. Skim excess fat off the liquid in the casserole, then boil rapidly until reduced by half. Mix the cream and egg yolks together in a small cup and add a little of the hot liquid to them. Pour it all back into the pan with half the parsley and whisk over a moderate heat (being careful that it doesn't boil) until it thickens. Taste and adjust the seasoning if necessary. Pour over the chicken and dust with the remaining parsley.

Serves 4–6

▼ 20 minutes   ◉ 20 minutes + 1 hour (oven)

Trinidad Chicken

A summer favourite which takes little time to make and always disappears very quickly.

3 oz (75g) seedless raisins
3 tablespoons rum
1/2 pint (275ml) thick
   homemade mayonnaise
6 tablespoons Green Label
   mango chutney
1 oz (25g) dessicated coconut
2 oz (50g) salted peanuts
2 tablespoons single or double
   cream

salt and pepper
2 large bananas
1 3 1/2-lb (1.5 kilos) chicken,
   cooked and cut into bite-size
   chunks
1 ripe avocado
a little lemon juice
chopped parsley or chervil

Put the raisins in a bowl, pour over the rum and leave to soak for several hours or overnight.

Put the mayonnaise into a large mixing bowl. Blend in the chutney, coconut, peanuts, raisins, rum and cream. Season to taste with salt and pepper. Chop one of the bananas and add to the mixture with the chicken. Taste and adjust the seasoning if necessary.*

Arrange the chicken in a serving dish. Cut the remaining banana and avocado into thin strips and arrange on top (squeeze a little lemon juice over them to prevent discoloration). Dust lightly with chopped chervil and serve with a rice or green salad.

Serves 6

 20 minutes   Marinating time: several hours or overnight
 to * ✳

Chicken Livers with Spinach and Bacon

1 oz (25g) butter
1/2 lb (225g) chicken livers,
   trimmed and ducts removed
salt and black pepper
2 rashers back bacon, diced

3/4 lb (350g) fresh young
   spinach, washed and stalks
   removed
a little lemon juice
a little freshly grated nutmeg

Melt the butter in a large, heavy pan and sauté the chicken livers quickly (they should be nicely browned but still pink inside). Season lightly, then lift out and keep warm.

Add the bacon dice to the same pan and cook quickly until the fat begins to run. Add the spinach, toss well in the juices and cook, stirring all the time, until it softens and cooks (this should take 3–5 minutes). Season well with a little lemon juice, grated nutmeg, salt and black pepper. Lift out and divide between two hot plates. Place the chicken livers on top and serve at once.

Serves 2

 10 minutes   ◉ 10 minutes   ✳

Turkey in Green Waistcoats

1½ oz (40g) butter
3 shallots, peeled and finely chopped
6 oz (175g) button mushrooms, finely diced
2 fl oz (50ml) dry white wine
salt and pepper
½ lb (225g) fresh spinach, well washed and drained
4 small turkey escalopes

Put ½ oz (15g) of butter into a medium pan and, when foaming, add the shallots. Sauté until soft and transparent, then add the remaining butter and the mushrooms. Continue cooking until the mushrooms have darkened, then add the white wine. Cook for about 5 minutes, then season to taste with salt and pepper. Put to one side.

Remove the stalks from the spinach, keeping the leaves intact. Blanch in gently simmering water for several minutes, then lift out. Refresh under cold running water, then spread carefully on kitchen paper and put to one side.

Put the escalopes, one at a time, between two sheets of cling-film and flatten with a rolling pin. Then cut a lengthwise 'pocket' in each one, being careful not to cut all the way through. Tuck a large dollop of the mushroom mixture into each pocket, then season the escalopes with salt and pepper. Wrap each one completely in spinach leaves, then wrap again in a parcel of foil. Place in a buttered baking dish* and bake in a preheated oven (450°F/Gas Mark 8/230°C) for 30 minutes. Take out, remove the foil and allow to cool slightly before serving. (Or cool completely in the foil and then serve cold.)

Serves 4

⬤ 15 minutes   ◨ about 20 minutes + 30 minutes (oven)
◖ to *

40

Curried Turkey Salad

If you prefer, cooked chicken could be used instead.

1½ lbs (675g) cooked turkey, chopped into medium chunks
2 oz (50g) almonds or peanuts
2 oz (50g) seedless raisins
4 oz (100g) fresh dates, stoned and sliced lengthwise
3 large stalks celery, finely diced
2 tablespoons chopped spring onion
3 tablespoons chopped red pepper

Curry Mayonnaise
10 level tablespoons mayonnaise
1 teaspoon Madras curry powder
4 tablespoons peach or mango chutney
1 tablespoon boiling water
2 tablespoons chopped fresh parsley
2 teaspoons lemon juice
salt and pepper

Start by making the curry mayonnaise. Measure the mayonnaise into a large mixing bowl and blend in the curry powder, chutney, boiling water, 1 tablespoon of parsley and the lemon juice. Season to taste with salt and pepper.

Add the other ingredients (reserving the parsley and 1 tablespoon of red pepper) and mix carefully. Taste and adjust the seasoning if necessary. Scatter the remaining parsley and red pepper over the top. Cover with cling-film until needed (but don't leave it longer than 2 hours).

Serves 4

⬤ 20 minutes   ✳

Meats

Supper, being the modest little meal that it is, does its best to use inexpensive cuts of meat. But without a sudden flash of inspiration, these inevitably end up as the all-too-familiar stew.

The barbecue provides one delicious alternative. This is no longer the fairweather sport it once was, for hooded grills and Hibachis small enough to use on a balcony or verandah are now available. Cheap cuts of beef, pork and lamb all thrive on an overnight marinade and then quick grill over the coals. Spareribs, chops and burgers have twice the flavour after a charcoal grilling. A simple marinade of lemon juice, oil, herbs, garlic and seasonings would suit pork, chicken and lamb. Beef needs a gutsier blend: red wine, shallots, red wine vinegar, oil and seasonings. A barbecue sauce (page 54) will perk up any grilled meat and soften what otherwise might be a charred exterior. But the addition of the sauce and subsequent basting should be done near the end of the cooking as it will burn if left on too long. Partially baked potatoes, sweetcorn and onions can be wrapped in foil and slipped in amongst the coals as the meat cooks.

Stir-frying is undoubtedly the best way to cook meat quickly without losing its juiciness. Braising or frying steak is marinated first, then sliced into thin strips and cooked quickly over a high heat in any large, heavy pan with fairly deep sides. Vegetables can be cooked in the pan first, then pushed to one side so the meat has room to brown.

Cheaper cuts of meat suit the extremes – a rapid grill, stir-fry or long, slow cooking. Casseroles and stews reduce tough meat to meltingly tender morsels – but the meat must first be browned quickly to seal in the flavour. After so many hours together in the same pot, the ingredients invariably come out with much the same consistency. Get round this by adding one of contrasting texture and colour (e.g., beans, broccoli, *mange-tout* peas) near the end of the cooking time. Leave the tomato purée on the shelf and vary the traditional formula. Dried fruits – peaches, pears, apricots, prunes – will add richness, while ale, cider, sherry, dry Martini, a little port or wine provide character. Resist the urge to add a sprig of rosemary: it will dominate the pot and, after a few hours, monopolize the flavour. Basil, oregano, marjoram, parsley and thyme are better choices – with perhaps just a scrap of bay leaf. For a spicy stew – ground coriander, cardamom seeds, nutmeg, ground cumin, cinnamon, chilli or curry powder – any of these would add interest. If you get fed up waiting for the stew, invest in a slow-cooker. It will cook all day – and be waiting for *you* in the evening.

Miss Moffat's Cottage Pie

1¹/₂ lbs (675g) lean minced beef *or* minced cooked beef or lamb
2 oz (50g) butter
1 medium onion, peeled and chopped
¹/₂ lb (225g) mushrooms, sliced
1 oz (25g) flour
¹/₂ pint (275ml) beef stock

1 tablespoon meat gravy *or* 1 teaspoon meat glaze or Bovril
1 tablespoon Worcestershire sauce
1 level tablespoon tomato purée
good pinch of brown sugar
salt and black pepper
¹/₂ lb (225g) peas

Topping
2 lbs (900g) potatoes, cooked
1¹/₂ oz (40g) butter
4 tablespoons milk

salt and pepper
freshly grated nutmeg

Brown the meat quickly in a large sauté or frying pan. Lift out and discard any fat. Add half the butter and sauté the onion until soft. Add the remaining butter with the mushrooms and cook until they darken. Stir in the flour and cook for several minutes. Then blend in the stock, meat gravy, Worcestershire sauce, tomato purée and brown sugar. Return the meat to the pan and season well with salt and pepper. Simmer for 10 minutes, add the peas, then transfer the mixture to a large baking dish.

Cream the potatoes with the milk and butter and season to taste with salt, pepper and nutmeg. Spread over the meat and rough up the top with a fork.* Bake at 350°F/Gas Mark 4/180°C for 45–60 minutes, or until lightly browned.

Serves 6

🝖 10–15 minutes ◙ 20 minutes + 45–60 minutes (oven) ◑ to * ⛰

Chilli con Carne

If you like your chilli blazing hot, make this with hot Italian sausage rather than the mild chorizo. If you can't find either, use a spicy pork sausage and increase the chilli powder.

1 oz (25g) butter
6 oz (175g) Spanish *chorizo* sausage *or* half hot sausage, half *chorizo*
6 oz (175g) finely chopped onion
1 small green pepper, chopped
1 lb (450g) lean minced beef
1 1³/₄-lb (793g) tin Italian tomatoes, with their juice

6 oz (175g) cooked kidney beans (if using tinned ones, drain well)
1 fat clove of garlic
1 tablespoon chilli powder
1 teaspoon ground cumin
salt and pepper

Melt the butter in a large, heavy sauté pan. Prick the sausage all over and brown quickly on all sides. Take out and cut into thin slices. Cook the onion and green pepper in the same pan until the onion is golden. Push to one side of the pan and add the meat. Brown it quickly, then add the tomatoes (and their juice) and break them up in the pan with the side of a wooden spoon. Then add the kidney beans, garlic, chilli powder, cumin, sausages and a good seasoning of salt and pepper. Mix well and simmer for an hour, stirring from time to time and having the occasional taste: if you want it hotter, add a bit more chilli powder; if it's too hot, add a good pinch of sugar and a little water. Serve piping hot on toasted baps (or on their own) with a very crisp green salad.

Serves 6

🝖 5 minutes ◙ 1¹/₄ hours

White's Moussaka

3/4 lb (350g) aubergine
salt
olive or vegetable oil
1 medium onion, peeled and
  finely chopped
1 lb (450g) coarsely minced
  raw lamb or beef

1 dessertspoon tomato purée
2–3 cloves of garlic, crushed
plenty of fresh herbs
pinch of ground allspice
black pepper
a little beef or lamb stock

Cheese Sauce
2 oz (50g) butter
2 oz (50g) flour

1 pint (575ml) milk
3 oz (75g) Cheddar, grated

Cut the aubergine in half lengthwise, then into thin slices crosswise. Salt well and, after 30 minutes, rinse and dry it. Heat several tablespoons of oil in a large sauté pan and fry the aubergine slices quickly on both sides, adding more oil when needed. Lift out and drain on kitchen paper.

Heat a little more oil and cook the onion and meat until the onion has softened. Stir in the tomato purée, garlic, fresh herbs, allspice, a good seasoning of salt and pepper, and enough stock to moisten the mixture.

To make the sauce, melt the butter in a small saucepan. Stir in the flour and cook for 1–2 minutes. Gradually blend in the milk and simmer gently, stirring all the time, until slightly thickened. Add the cheese and gently melt it, then season to taste.

Preheat the oven to 400°F/Gas Mark 6/200°C. Build up layers of aubergine, meat and cheese sauce in an ovenproof dish, ending with sauce. Bake until brown and bubbling (about 45 minutes). Serve with a crisp green salad.

Serves 4

⬤ 45 minutes ▣ 30 minutes + 45 minutes (oven) ◐ ▲▲

Schmaltzburgers

For when you want to make hamburgers seem less of a snack and more of a meal.

1 lb (450g) lean minced beef
4 oz (100g) finely chopped
  onion *or* 4 spring onions,
  finely chopped
3 back bacon rashers, cooked
  until crisp and diced
1 teaspoon French mustard
2 teaspoons Worcestershire
  sauce

1 slice of bread, crusts
  removed
salt and black pepper
1 egg, lightly beaten
4 oz (100g) good Cheddar,
  grated
4 large baps
1 large ripe tomato, sliced
a few crisp lettuce leaves

In a large mixing bowl, mash the beef slightly with a fork, then add the onion and bacon. Blend the mustard with the Worcestershire sauce, then mix in. Crumble the bread into crumbs and add with a generous seasoning of salt and pepper. Bind together with the beaten egg.

Divide the mixture into eight neat patties. Divide the cheese between four of them, then top with the remaining four and press down firmly. Enclose the cheese completely by pressing the sides of the top patty down over the bottom one. Shape into neat rounds.

Cook the schmaltzburgers over a barbecue (by far the best way to bring out their flavour) or under a hot grill until done the way you like them, flipping them over halfway. Take out and transfer to warm baps. Place a tomato slice and crisp lettuce leaf on top of each 'burger', add whatever mustard or relish you fancy and eat at once.

Serves 4, or 2 ravenous eaters

⬤ 10 minutes ▣ 10 minutes  ◐   ▲▲   ✶

Carpetbag Steak

This produces meltingly tender meat with little effort by the cook.

2 braising steaks
a little seasoned flour
1¹/₂ oz (40g) butter
1 medium onion, peeled and
  sliced
¹/₂ large red pepper, cut into
  thin strips
¹/₄ lb (100g) button
  mushrooms
salt and pepper
6 tablespoons red wine

Toss the steaks in the seasoned flour until well coated, then shake off any excess.

Heat 1 oz (25g) of the butter in a large sauté or frying pan and, when hot, brown the steaks quickly on both sides. Lift out and put to one side. Add the onion and pepper and cook for about 5 minutes. Add the mushrooms and cook quickly until they have darkened in colour but not softened. Season well with salt and black pepper.

Take a long length of foil (about 4 times the width of the steak) and fold in half. Cut it so that when opened it forms a heart shape. Place it shiny side down on the work top and spread half the remaining butter all over inside. Put the steak in the middle of one half and cover with half the onion/mushroom mixture. Season lightly with salt and pepper. Carefully pour over 3 tablespoons of red wine. Fold the foil over, pinch the edges together to seal and crimp tightly. Do the same with the other steak. Place both parcels on a baking sheet,* put into a preheated oven (350°F/Gas Mark 4/180°C) and cook for 1–1¹/₂ hours. Take out and transfer the contents of each parcel to hot plates.

Serves 2

● 10 minutes ◖ 15 minutes + 1–1¹/₂ hours (oven) ◑ to *

Beef Teriyaki

You could make a 'teriyaki' equally well with thinly sliced pork or chicken.

1 scant tablespoon finely
  grated fresh ginger *or* 1
  scant teaspoon ground
  ginger
1 shallot or button onion,
  peeled and finely chopped
1 clove of garlic, peeled and
  crushed
2 fl oz (50ml) soy sauce
2 fl oz (50ml) dry sherry
1 tablespoon brown sugar
1 lb (450g) rump or braising
  steak

Mix the ginger, shallot, garlic, soy sauce, sherry and brown sugar together in a small bowl. Stir until the sugar has dissolved.

Place the steak on a large plate and completely cover with the soy sauce marinade. Leave for several hours at room temperature, turning the steak over every hour.

When ready to cook the steak, pour off the marinade. Place the steak on a piece of foil in the grill pan. When the grill is very hot, put the steak 2–3 inches (5–7.5cm) underneath it. Cook quickly on both sides, so that the steak is still pink inside. Take out, cut into diagonal slices and serve with spiced rice and salad.

Serves 3

● 5 minutes   Marinating time: several hours ◖ 5 minutes
◑

Beef with Leeks and Spring Onions

³/₄ lb (350g) braising steak
1 oz (25g) flour
salt and pepper
1 oz (25g) butter
2 tablespoons vegetable oil
3 slices root ginger, peeled and finely chopped
³/₄ lb (350g) leeks, washed and shredded

10 oz (275g) bean sprouts or French beans
1 large spring onion, chopped
2 tablespoons soy sauce
¹/₄ pint (150ml) beef stock
1¹/₂ teaspoons sugar
salt and pepper

Cut the beef into thin strips. Mix the flour with a good seasoning of salt and black pepper. Toss the beef strips in it until well coated, then shake off the excess.

Heat the butter and oil in the largest, heaviest sauté pan you can find. When very hot, add the ginger and beef and stir-fry over a high heat until the beef is nicely browned. Add the leeks, sprouts, spring onion, soy sauce, stock and sugar. Mix and leave to cook for 2–4 minutes longer. Season to taste with salt and pepper and stir well. Serve with lots of fluffy white rice.

Serves 3–4

🍴 15 minutes   ◉ 8 minutes   ✱

Beef Stew with Orange

1¹/₂ oz (40g) butter
1 tablespoon olive or vegetable oil
2 lbs (900g) stewing beef
1 medium onion, peeled and finely chopped
2 rashers back bacon, finely diced

2 level tablespoons plain flour
1¹/₂ pints (850ml) beef stock
rind of 1 orange
juice of 2 oranges
6 oz (175g) prunes
2 tablespoons chopped parsley
salt and pepper
1 teaspoon white wine vinegar

Heat the butter and oil in a large, flameproof casserole. Trim the meat and cut into medium pieces. Brown quickly (do in several lots, rather than crowd the pan), then lift out with a slotted spoon. Add the onion and bacon to the pan and cook slowly until the onion is golden.

Stir in the flour and cook for a minute. Blend in the stock, orange rind, orange juice, prunes and half the parsley. Season well with salt and pepper and bring up to the boil. Cover and put into a preheated oven (325°F/Gas Mark 3/170°C) and cook for 1³/₄ hours. Take out, add the vinegar and give it a good stir. Cook uncovered for a further 15–20 minutes. Check the seasoning and adjust if necessary. Scatter the remaining parsley over the top and serve with boiled potatoes and salad.

Serves 4

🍴 15 minutes   ◉ 20 minutes + 2 hours (oven)   ◗   ▲▲

Liver with Sage and Bacon

Very quick and easy, with a flavour which belies its simplicity.

2¹/₂ oz (65g) butter
2 rashers back bacon
3 large sprigs fresh sage
2 large very thin slices calves'
   liver

¹/₄ pint (150ml) beef stock
good squeeze of lemon juice
pepper

Melt ¹/₂ oz (15g) of butter in a large, heavy sauté or frying pan. Add the bacon and sage and cook slowly until the bacon is crisp. Lift the rashers out with a slotted spoon, leaving the sage in the pan.

Melt the remaining butter in the pan and, when very hot, add the calves' liver. Cook very quickly (it should be seared first on both sides to seal in the juices) until browned but still pink inside, spooning the pan juices over occasionally.

Transfer the liver to hot plates with the bacon, cover and keep warm. Pour the stock into the pan and boil rapidly (scraping the bottom of the pan at the same time) for a minute or two until slightly thickened. Add a squeeze of lemon juice and black pepper. Pour this lovely *jus* over the liver and eat at once.

Serves 2

◉ 10 minutes ✱

46

Spring Lamb Stew

2 lbs (900g) middle neck of
   lamb
2 oz (50g) butter
8 oz (225g) finely sliced onion
1 lb (450g) carrots, peeled and
   cut into 2-inch (5cm)
   matchsticks
1 level teaspoon castor sugar

¹/₂ oz (15g) flour
1 level tablespoon tomato
   purée
1 pint (575ml) beef stock
salt and pepper
2 tablespoons finely chopped
   parsley
1 14-oz (400g) tin *petits pois*

Trim the meat neatly, removing any excess fat or bone. Melt the butter in a large flameproof casserole and brown the meat quickly on both sides. Transfer to a plate and put to one side. Add the onion and carrots to the casserole with the sugar and toss well in the buttery juices. Cook over moderate heat, stirring from time to time, until the onion is just beginning to brown. Sprinkle the flour on top, stir and cook for a minute or two. Add the tomato purée and stock, then stir carefully until well blended. Season lightly with salt and pepper, add half the parsley and bring up to the boil. Return the meat to the pan, cover and put the pot into a preheated oven (350°F/Gas Mark 4/180°C) for 1¹/₄ hours.

Take the casserole out and gently stir in the *petits pois* with 1 tablespoon of their juice. Return (covered) to the oven and continue cooking for a further 45 minutes. Check the seasoning, and scatter the remaining parsley over the top. Serve warm with boiled or jacket potatoes.

Serves 6

◗ 15 minutes ◉ 20 minutes + 2 hours (oven)

Epigrams of Lamb

2 breasts of lamb (2¹/₂–3 lbs/1–1.5 kilos total weight)	salt, pepper
1 large onion, peeled	water
2 large leeks, cleaned	1 egg, lightly beaten
3 large carrots, peeled	6 tablespoons dried white breadcrumbs
6 peppercorns	2 oz (50g) unsalted butter
small bay leaf	2–3 tablespoons vegetable oil

Remove as much fat as possible from the breasts, then place in a large pot. Chop the vegetables roughly then add to the pot with the peppercorns, bay leaf and good seasoning of salt and pepper. Pour in enough cold water to cover the lamb and bring to the boil. Skim off any scum, then cover and simmer gently for 1¹/₂ hours.

Lift the lamb out and allow to cool slightly. (Strain the stock and save to make soup.) Pull out all the bones from the meat and trim off any obvious fat. Place the meat between layers of kitchen paper and two bread boards and weight the top. Leave for several hours, until cold and flattened.

Remove the boards and paper, then cut the meat into neat rectangles about 3 inches (7.5cm) long. Dip each piece in the beaten egg, then coat well with breadcrumbs. Put to one side* for 10–15 minutes, then heat the butter and oil in a large, heavy pan. Fry the epigrams for 5–10 minutes each side, until golden brown. Lift out, drain on kitchen paper and serve with lots of mashed potatoes.

Serves 4

 20 minutes   2 hours   Cooling time: 2 hours
 to *

Lamb Chops with Mint Butter

6 good-sized lamb chops

Mint Butter

4 oz (100g) soft butter	1 teaspoon lemon juice
3 tablespoons finely chopped fresh mint (2 tablespoons if using dried)	1¹/₂ teaspoons orange juice
	salt and black pepper

Cream the butter in a large mixing bowl until light. Beat in the mint (if using dried, crumble it between your fingers to release the flavour), lemon and orange juice, salt and pepper. When well blended, shape into a small log about 1 inch (2.5cm) in diameter. Wrap in greaseproof paper or foil and chill until firm.* (Bring to room temperature before serving.)

Grill the lamb chops until they are as pink or as 'done' as you like them. Transfer to hot plates and place two thin slices of the mint butter on each chop. Serve with baked potatoes (which could also get a dollop of mint butter if there's any left) and a crunchy vegetable – perhaps carrots or broccoli.

Serves 6

 15 minutes   Chilling time: 30–45 minutes   15 minutes
 to *

47

Lamb with Rice, Spices and Nuts

1 lb (450g) boned lamb
2 oz (50g) butter
1 medium onion, peeled and chopped
1 medium green pepper, finely chopped
6^1/$_2$ oz (190g) long-grain rice
^{1}/$_4$ teaspoon ground cinnamon
^{1}/$_4$ teaspoon mixed spice
generous grating of nutmeg
^{3}/$_4$ pint (425ml) beef or lamb stock
salt and black pepper
2 tablespoons chopped parsley
2 oz (50g) toasted pine nuts or flaked almonds

Cut the lamb into medium chunks, removing any excess fat. Heat 1^1/$_2$ oz (40g) butter in a large sauté pan with a lid (or flameproof casserole) and brown the lamb quickly. Push to one side of the pan and add the onion and pepper. Stir until well coated in the butter, then cook until the onion is golden.

Melt the remaining butter in the pan, then stir in the rice and spices. Cook for a minute or two, until the rice becomes translucent. Then add the stock, a good seasoning of salt and pepper and half the parsley. Stir once and bring up to the boil. Cover, reduce the heat and simmer gently for 25–30 minutes, or until all the liquid has been absorbed. Remove from the heat and leave (covered) to steam for 10–15 minutes. Then uncover, check the seasoning and, if necessary, add more spice, salt or pepper. Fork into a hot serving dish and scatter the toasted nuts and remaining parsley on top. Serve with a green salad.

Serves 4

◗ 15 minutes   ◙ 45 minutes   Steaming: 10 minutes   ◕

48

Kidneys with Creamy Mustard Sauce

2 oz (50g) butter
2 lbs (900g) lambs' kidneys, skinned, trimmed and halved

Creamy Mustard Sauce
1 oz (25g) butter
6 button onions, peeled and quartered
^{1}/$_4$ pint (150ml) dry cider
2 level tablespoons Dijon mustard
4 level tablespoons soft butter
1–2 tablespoons cider or white vinegar
1 tablespoon chopped parsley
salt and pepper

Melt 2 oz butter in a heavy sauté pan and cook the kidneys until lightly browned, but still slightly pink inside. Transfer to a large plate, reverse another one on top and keep in a warm oven until the sauce is ready.

Melt 1 oz butter in a small saucepan and sauté the onions until soft and transparent. Pour in the cider and boil rapidly until reduced by half. Mix the mustard and soft butter together until you have a smooth paste. Take the pan off the heat and whisk in the mustard butter, small pieces at a time, until the sauce is thick and glossy. Sharpen with a little vinegar, then add half the parsley and season to taste with salt and pepper. Put over a very low heat until hot again, then pour over the kidneys, scatter the remaining parsley on top and serve.

Serves 4

◗ 10 minutes   ◙ 15 minutes   ✱

Devilled Lamb Chops

4 large lamb chump chops

Devil Sauce

3 tablespoons Dijon mustard	1 oz (25g) melted butter
3 tablespoons Worcestershire sauce	salt and pepper to taste
2 tablespoons peach or mango chutney	2 tablespoons dry sherry

Mix all the devil ingredients in a small bowl until smooth and well blended.*

Arrange the chops in a shallow baking tin and coat with the devil sauce. Put under a hot grill (not too close) for about 5 minutes. Flip over and coat with more sauce. Continue grilling until the chops are cooked as you like them. Take out, coat with the pan juices and serve with crisp watercress (if you have it to hand).

Serves 4

⬤ 5 minutes   ◼ 10 minutes   ◗ to *   ✱

Kidneys in Baked Potatoes

2 large potatoes	1¹/₂ oz (40g) butter
6 rashers streaky bacon, rinds removed	3 large kidneys, halved
	salt and black pepper

Scrub the potatoes well, then prick in several places with a fork and insert a skewer into the middle of each one. Bake in a hot oven (400°F/Gas Mark 6/200°C) for about 1¹/₄ hours or until tender. (Leave the oven on.)

Grill the bacon until almost crisp and put to one side. Melt 1 oz (25g) of the butter in a heavy pan and sauté the kidneys quickly, until nicely browned but still slightly pink inside. Lift out with a slotted spoon and reserve the pan juices. When cool enough to handle, wrap each one in a bacon rasher.

Take the potatoes out of the oven and cut a large, deep circle out of the top. Remove most of the potato on the underside of the 'lids'. There should now be enough room inside each potato to put a row of three bacon-wrapped kidneys. (If there isn't, scoop out a little more potato.) Season the inside of the potatoes well with salt and black pepper; then pour in the juices from the kidney pan and spread with the remaining butter. Put the kidneys in a row of three in each potato, then replace the lids. Wrap each potato in foil and bake in a hot oven (temperature as above) for about 20 minutes. Take out, remove the foil, allow to cool slightly, then eat at once.

Serves 2

⬤ 10 minutes   ◼ 10 minutes + 1¹/₂ hours (oven)

Veal with Soured Cream and Mushrooms

If you reheat this, do so with care. Soured cream reacts violently to anything more energetic than a slow simmer.

2 lbs (900g) pie veal
3 oz (75g) butter
4 oz (100g) onion, peeled and finely sliced
1/2 lb (225g) button mushrooms, thickly sliced
2 level tablespoons flour
1/2 pint (275ml) soured cream
salt and pepper
1 tablespoon finely chopped parsley
2 teaspoons lemon juice

Cut the veal into 1-inch (2.5cm) cubes and remove any fat. Heat 1 1/2 oz (40g) butter in a large flameproof casserole and brown the veal quickly (do this in several lots), then lift out with a slotted spoon. Add the onion and cook until golden. Add another 1/2 oz (15g) butter to the pan with the mushrooms and cook quickly for several minutes. Lift the vegetables out of the pan with a slotted spoon and put with the veal.

Heat the remaining butter in the pan and stir in the flour. Cook for a minute, then take off the heat and blend in the soured cream, scraping the bottom of the pan to loosen the brown sediment. Return to moderate heat and stir for several minutes (it will be very thick). Tip the veal, onions, mushrooms and their juice back into the pan. Blend well and give a good seasoning of salt and black pepper.* Cover and put into a preheated oven (325°F/Gas Mark 3/170°C) for 1 1/2 hours or until the meat is tender when pierced with a skewer. After an hour, take the pot out, add most of the parsley and all the lemon juice and stir well. Cover and return to the oven. Just before serving, check the seasoning and dust with parsley. Serve with rice or noodles and a salad.

Serves 4

🥄 10 minutes ◉ 20 minutes + 1 1/2 hours (oven) ◐ to *

50

Veal or Pork with Lemon

2 veal escalopes *or* 1 small pork fillet
seasoned flour
2 tablespoons olive or vegetable oil
2 oz (50g) butter
5 fl oz (150ml) dry white wine
2 tablespoons lemon juice
salt and pepper
pinch of sugar (if needed)
2 teaspoons finely chopped parsley or chervil

Pound the escalopes very flat (or have the butcher do this for you), then cut into squares about 1 1/2 inches (3.5cm). (If using pork fillet instead, cut into slices crosswise, pound flat, then cut in half to make semi-circles.) Dip the squares in seasoned flour until well coated, then shake off any excess.

Heat the oil and half the butter in a large, heavy pan. Cook the veal quickly (don't crowd the pan, cook in two batches if necessary) until golden brown on both sides. Lift out with a fish slice and keep warm in the oven.

Pour the wine into the pan and scrape the bottom vigorously to loosen the sediment. Continue to whisk the mixture over a gentle heat until it has reduced by almost half. Take the pan off the heat and whisk in the lemon juice, then the remaining butter, small pieces at a time. Season to taste with salt and pepper. If too sharp, add a pinch of sugar. Scatter the parsley over the top and put the pan back over a low heat for several minutes (but don't let it boil). Transfer the meat to a hot serving dish, pour the sauce over it and serve with crisp French beans and perhaps a little hot rice or noodles.

Serves 2

🥄 15 minutes ◉ 15 minutes ✱

Creamy Veal with Carrots

1 lb (450g) lean pie veal, cut into ¹/₂-inch (1cm) cubes
¹/₂ lb (225g) carrots, peeled and cut into thin strips
¹/₂ lb (225g) button onions, peeled
sprig of parsley
¹/₂ pint (275ml) chicken stock
salt and pepper
1 oz (25g) butter
1 oz (25g) flour
1 egg yolk
4 fl oz (100ml) double cream
good squeeze of lemon juice
1 tablespoon finely chopped parsley

Put the veal, carrots, onions, sprig of parsley, chicken stock, a little salt and pepper into a medium saucepan. Bring to the boil, then cover and cook very gently until the veal is tender (40–60 minutes). Strain the liquid into a jug and put to one side. Tip the contents of the sieve (minus the parsley) into a bowl.

In another saucepan, melt the butter and stir in the flour. Cook for a minute or two, then take off the heat and gradually blend in the liquid from the veal. Simmer for several minutes, stirring continuously until the sauce is smooth and shiny. Blend in the vegetables and veal. Mix the yolk and cream together in a small cup, add a little of the hot sauce, then tip it all back into the pot. Add a good squeeze of lemon juice, the chopped parsley and salt and pepper to taste. Heat very gently, being careful not to let it boil. Delicious served with boiled new potatoes and peas.

Serves 4

 15 minutes   1¹/₄ hours   ◀

Pork with Cider and Spices

1¹/₂ lbs (675g) pork fillet
¹/₂ teaspoon ground ginger
¹/₄ teaspoon ground cinnamon
¹/₂ teaspoon ground mixed spice
pinch of cayenne pepper
2 oz (50g) butter
1 tablespoon olive or vegetable oil
¹/₂ medium onion, peeled and finely sliced
¹/₂ large green pepper, finely sliced
¹/₂ lb (225g) button mushrooms, thickly sliced
¹/₄ pint (150ml) dry cider
¹/₄ pint (150ml) double cream
salt and pepper
a little lemon juice to sharpen (if needed)

Cut across the pork fillet into slices ¹/₄ inch (.50cm) thick and then into thin strips. Mix the spices together on a large plate, then add the pork strips and toss until well coated.

Heat the butter and oil in a large, heavy sauté or frying pan. Add the onion and pepper and gently sauté until the onion is golden. Push to one side of the pan and add the pork. Brown very quickly over high heat, then add the mushrooms and cook for several minutes longer. Pour in the cider and simmer gently until it has reduced by a third. Reduce the heat and blend in the cream. Season with salt and pepper and a little lemon juice to sharpen (if needed). Heat very gently until the sauce thickens. Serve with plain or spiced rice and a green salad.

Serves 4

 15 minutes   25 minutes

Sweet and Sour Pork

3 tablespoons vegetable oil
1 medium onion, peeled and
  finely sliced
3 slices of fresh ginger, peeled
  and chopped, *or* 1¹/₂
  teaspoons ground ginger
1¹/₂ lbs (675g) lean boneless
  pork cut into medium
  chunks

1 medium green pepper, thinly
  sliced
1 8-oz (225g) tin pineapple
  chunks, drained of juice

Sweet and Sour Sauce
2 level tablespoons cornflour
3¹/₂ tablespoons brown sugar
4 tablespoons vinegar
1 tablespoon thick honey
2 tablespoons soy sauce

3 tablespoons orange juice
5 fl oz (150ml) pineapple
  syrup
5 fl oz (150ml) water
salt and pepper to taste

Mix all the ingredients for the sweet and sour sauce in the order they are given. Put to one side.

Heat the oil in a large, heavy sauté or frying pan. Add the onion and ginger and stir-fry for several minutes. Add the pork and green pepper and continue to stir-fry for 4–5 minutes. Pour in the sauce with the pineapple chunks and cook, stirring all the time, over a moderately high heat until it thickens. Simmer gently for several minutes, then serve with fluffy white rice and a crisp green salad.

Serves 4

 15 minutes   ◉ 10 minutes   ◖

Pork Boulangère

2 large pork chops
2¹/₂ oz (65g) butter
¹/₂ large onion, peeled and
  sliced
1 fat clove of garlic, crushed
salt and black pepper
1 large slice cooked ham *or* 2
  rashers back bacon, grilled
  until crisp

chopped chives or parsley
6 small new potatoes, well
  scrubbed
6 tablespoons cider or beef
  stock

Trim the pork chops of excess fat and wipe dry with kitchen paper. Melt 2 oz (50g) of butter in a large frying pan and, when foaming, add the chops. Brown quickly on both sides, then lift out. Add the onion and garlic and cook until golden.

Cut out two large heart-shapes in foil. Open each one, putting the shiny side down on the work surface. Rub the remaining butter all over the inside of the foil (being careful not to tear it with your nails). Place each chop in the centre of one half of the heart. Season well with salt and black pepper. Cover with the onions and garlic and any buttery juices in the pan. Shred the ham (or crumble the bacon) and place on top with a little chopped parsley or chives. Cut the potatoes in half and put round the chops. Pour 3 tablespoons of cider or stock over each one and fold over the foil to enclose completely. Pinch the edges to seal and crimp tightly. Put the packets on a baking tray* and into a preheated oven (350°F/Gas Mark 4/180°C). Cook for an hour (or until the pork is tender). Take out and place the parcels on individual plates. Take to the table, slash open and peel back the foil.

Serves 2

 10 minutes   ◉ 15 minutes + 1 hour (oven)   to *

Pork with Parsnip Purée

1 lb (450g) parsnips, peeled and chopped
salt and pepper
1 oz (25g) butter
grating of nutmeg
pinch of dry mustard

1 tablespoon single cream
2 oz (50g) good Cheddar, grated
2 large pork chops
chopped chervil or parsley

Put the chopped parsnips into a large saucepan with salt and very little water. Cover and cook rapidly until tender. Drain well, then mash with the butter until smooth. Season well with salt and freshly ground black pepper, then add a good grating of nutmeg, generous pinch of dry mustard, the single cream and half the cheese.

While the parsnips are cooking, grill the chops well on both sides. Arrange the mashed parsnip in the bottom of a lightly buttered gratin or ovenproof dish and place the chops on top, pressing them down well. Scatter the remaining cheese and a little chopped chervil or parsley on top.* Put into a preheated oven (350°F/Gas Mark 4/180°C) and bake for 20–30 minutes or until the pork is cooked through. Serve with crisp French beans or salad.

Pork Chops with Gruyère and Mustard

Don't cheat by using Cheddar – it's the Gruyère that makes this recipe so delicious.

¹/₂ oz (15g) butter
1 tablespoon olive or vegetable oil
4 thick pork chops
4 oz (100g) Gruyère, grated

2 teaspoons Dijon mustard
4–5 tablespoons double cream
salt and pepper
chopped parsley

Heat the butter and oil in a large frying pan and, when very hot, add the chops and brown quickly on both sides. Cover, reduce the heat and cook over moderate heat until cooked through.

Mix the cheese, mustard and cream together in a small bowl. Season the chops well, then place in a grill pan. Coat with the mustardy mixture and grill for 3–5 minutes, or until bubbly and lightly browned. Give a light dusting of chopped parsley and serve.

Serves 2

🥄 5 minutes   🍲 15 minutes + 30 minutes (oven)   ◖ to *

Serves 4

🥄 5 minutes   🍲 20 minutes   ✽

SC - D✳

53

Spareribs with Ginger and Honey

1½–2 lbs (675g–1 kilo) pork spareribs (American cut)

Ginger and Honey Sauce

1½ teaspoons soy sauce	1 teaspoon ground ginger
2 tablespoons mango chutney	1 clove of garlic, crushed
4 tablespoons lemon juice	1 tablespoon vegetable oil
6 tablespoons thick honey	2 tablespoons dry sherry

Put all the sauce ingredients into a small saucepan. Stir until well blended, then bring to the boil. Reduce the heat and simmer gently for about 10 minutes. Take off the heat and put to one side.

Line a large roasting tin with foil and put the ribs on top. Coat with the sauce and leave to marinate for several hours, turning them over whenever you think of it.*

When ready to cook the spareribs, lift them out of the tin and place on a large rack. Tip the marinade out of the roasting tin and put in a small bowl. Return the rack and ribs to the roasting tin and brush lightly with the marinade. Put into a preheated oven (350°F/Gas Mark 4/180°C) and bake for an hour, brushing with more sauce every 15 minutes and basting with the juices in the tin (flip the ribs over halfway through the cooking time). Take out, cut the ribs into 'fingers' and put on a serving dish (or individual plates). Coat with the pan juices (skim off any fat first) and serve.

Serves 4

◖ 5 minutes   Marinating time: 2 hours or overnight
◙ 10 minutes + 1 hour (oven)   ◕ to *

54

Pork with Barbecue Sauce

2 lbs (900g) pork chops or American-cut spareribs

Barbecue Sauce

1 oz (25g) butter	2 tablespoons sherry
1 small onion, peeled and finely chopped	1 tablespoon brown sugar
4 tablespoons tomato ketchup	2 tablespoons cider or wine vinegar
1 tablespoon thick honey	salt and pepper
1 tablespoon soy sauce	6 fl oz (175ml) water
1 tablespoon Worcestershire sauce	

Start by making the sauce. Melt the butter in a medium saucepan and sauté the onion until soft and transparent. Add all the remaining sauce ingredients and stir until well blended. Bring to the boil, then reduce the heat and simmer gently until the mixture is thick and syrupy (coating consistency). Take off the heat, season to taste and add a little extra vinegar if necessary to sharpen.*

Line a large roasting tin with foil. Put the chops or spareribs on it and coat with a generous amount of the sauce. Cover the tin and bake in a preheated oven (375°F/Gas Mark 5/190°C) for 20 minutes. Take out, turn the meat over and coat with more of the sauce. Cook uncovered for a further 20–30 minutes, basting frequently. Take the meat out, transfer to a hot serving dish. Skim the fat off the juices in the tin, then pour the juices over the pork. Serve with a crisp green salad.

Serves 4

◖ 15 minutes   ◙ 15 minutes + 50 minutes (oven)
◕ to *

Porkers with Red Cabbage

8 large old-fashioned pork sausages

Red Cabbage

1/2 red cabbage	5 tablespoons water
1/2 large onion	1 tablespoon brown sugar
2 large dessert apples	1/2 tablespoon redcurrant jelly
handful of raisins	salt and pepper
3 tablespoons red wine vinegar	

Shred the cabbage, then peel the onion and slice thinly. Peel the apples, quarter and remove the core. Then cut into thickish slices. Put the cabbage, onion, apples and raisins into a large, heavy saucepan and sprinkle the wine vinegar, water and brown sugar over them. Mix well, then cover and cook over a moderate heat for about an hour, shaking the pan from time to time to prevent sticking. (The cabbage should be *al dente*, not soggy.) Near the end of the cooking time, mix in the redcurrant jelly and add a good seasoning of salt and pepper. When the cabbage is ready, taste and add more seasoning or vinegar to sharpen if needed.*

Grill the sausages and dish up with the red cabbage and a steaming mound of mashed potatoes.

Serves 4

 5 minutes   1 hour   ◀ to *

Grilled Ham with Melon

This recipe's rapido *sauce goes magically with the ham.*

3 oz (75g) peach chutney	1/2 ripe honeydew melon, rind
1/2 teaspoon curry powder	removed and cut into thin
1 tablespoon lemon juice	wedges, lengthwise
2 oz (50g) butter	juice of 1/2 lemon
4 large slices cooked ham, cut	
1/8 inch (.25cm) thick	

Put the chutney, curry powder and lemon juice into a liquidizer or food processor. Blend until smooth. Melt the butter (being careful to *just* melt it, don't let it get hot) and add slowly to the chutney mixture. Transfer to a small bowl, cover and leave until needed.*

When ready to serve the ham, heat the grill. Cover a grill pan with foil and place the ham slices on it. Coat with a little of the chutney mixture and grill until bubbling and lightly browned. Flip over, coat with more of the mixture and grill until bubbling again. Transfer to hot plates and keep warm. Place the melon wedges on the foil, squeeze the lemon juice over them and put under the grill for a minute. Arrange on the plates with the ham and coat the ham with the pan juices. Serve with crisp watercress or a green salad.

Serves 4

 10 minutes   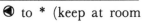 10 minutes   ◀ to * (keep at room temperature)

Ham with Cider and Raisin Sauce

A recipe inherited from my grandmother but never quite so good as when she made it.

8 large slices cooked honey-roast ham

Cider and Raisin Sauce

1/2 teaspoon dry English mustard	3 oz (75g) seedless raisins
1 1/2 level tablespoons cornflour	8 cloves
	1/4 teaspoon ground cinnamon
2 oz (50g) soft brown sugar	good pinch of ground nutmeg
3/4 pint (425ml) dry cider	salt

Wrap the ham in foil and put in a warm oven while you make the sauce.

Mix the mustard, cornflour and brown sugar together in a medium saucepan. Gradually blend in the cider, then add the raisins and spices. Stir over moderate heat until the mixture boils. Then reduce the heat and simmer gently until thick, shiny and syrupy (stirring frequently). Season to taste with a little salt. Transfer the ham to individual plates, coat with a little of the sauce and serve the rest separately.

Serves 4

━ 5 minutes ◨ 10 minutes ◖ ✱

Virginia Baked Ham

1 4-lb (2 kilos) corner end of gammon, soaked for several hours in cold water	1 8-oz (225g) tin pineapple slices
	4 glacé or cocktail cherries
	whole cloves

Glaze

1 tablespoon French mustard	large pinch of ground mixed spice
3 oz (75g) soft brown sugar	
2 tablespoons thick honey	1 teaspoon orange juice
large pinch of ground cloves	1 teaspoon wine vinegar

Drain the gammon, wrap it in foil and place, fat side up, in a medium roasting tin. Bake in a preheated oven (350°F/Gas Mark 4/180°C) for about 2 hours, allowing 30 minutes per pound.*

Mix the mustard and brown sugar together, then gradually add the honey, spices, orange juice and vinegar, to make a smooth paste.

Take the gammon out of the oven and peel pack the foil. Press it down firmly against the base and sides of the tin. Using a sharp, serrated knife, slice off the outer rind and discard. Slash the fat all over in a diamond-shaped pattern. Spread the sauce evenly over the joint, pressing it well into the fat. Decorate with pineapple slices and the cherries, halved. Secure them with toothpicks cut in half. Stud any 'diamonds' not covered with a whole clove. Bake the gammon for a further 45 minutes or until nicely browned, basting frequently with the pan juices, adding a little water if it gets too thick. Cool slightly, then serve with scalloped potatoes (or serve cold with baked potatoes and salad).

Serves 8

Soaking time: at least 3 hours ━ 10 minutes ◨ 2 3/4 hours ◖ to *

Fish

Brillat-Savarin once remarked that 'in the hands of an able cook, fish can become an inexhaustible source of perpetual delight.' Provided, of course, that the cook is inexhaustible as well.

When time or energy is in short supply, the easiest way to cook fish is in a paper or foil parcel. Buy the fish filleted or cleaned so that it needs no preparation. Butter a large piece of foil (or greaseproof paper) and place the fish on it. Season well, add a sprig of tarragon or parsley and a few generous knobs of butter. Seal and bake in a moderate oven for 20–30 minutes (depending on the size of the fish). If this seems too prosaic, add julienne strips of carrot, leek and courgette or lightly sautéed mushrooms and onions. Several spoonfuls of dry Martini, white wine or double cream will provide the fish with its own ready-made sauce. A gentle squeeze of lemon juice will bring out the flavour.

Baking without the foil or paper wrap is also quick and effective. Haddock fillets coated in a mixture of breadcrumbs, sesame seeds and melted butter emerge from the oven crisp and golden brown. Poppy or sunflower seeds could be substituted with equally good results.

There are obvious wallflowers at the fishmonger's and monkfish is one of them. Wrongly so, for it has tremendous character and flavour – with a texture similiar to that of scampi. It can be cooked like scallops, in butter and breadcrumbs, or like lobster *à l'Américaine*. In her classic *Fish Cookery*, Jane Grigson gives an excellent recipe in which monkfish tails are rolled in crushed peppercorns, sautéed in butter, then finished with a port and cream sauce. It may sound indigestible but is, in fact, sensational.

Haddock, monkfish, halibut and plaice all do well *en brochette*. String them on a skewer with mushrooms, bacon or pieces of mango. Brush with a little melted butter, roll in dried breadcrumbs or toasted poppy (or sesame) seeds and grill. To give a slightly different flavour, marinate them for a few hours in a blend of lime juice, ground coriander and oil.

Smoked fish is a good standby for last-minute dishes and always comes to the rescue just as panic is about to set in. Haddock suits any creamy sauce; mackerel needs something sharper to offset its richness – a mustard sauce, gooseberry purée or crisp apple salad. Frozen smoked fish fillets are actually rather good, and indispensable when making a spur-of-the-moment omelette Arnold Bennett.

A plainly grilled, fried or baked fish needs only the simplest of sauces. Aioli – that thick, garlicky mayonnaise – can be made in minutes and brings cod, haddock or plaice dramatically to life. A béchamel sauce, spiked with lemon juice, chopped cucumber or watercress, is an easy way to make ordinary fish seem rather posh.

Mackerel with Mustard and Herb Sauce

This has a lovely green and gold sauce which can be made easily at the last minute – or up to an hour before it's needed if kept over a pan of hot water.

4 fresh mackerel, cleaned and gutted

Mustard and Herb Sauce

2 egg yolks
1 scant tablespoon pale Dijon
  mustard
1 generous tablespoon
  chopped herbs (parsley,
  tarragon, chives)

2 oz (50g) unsalted butter, at
  room temperature
squeeze of lemon juice
salt and black pepper

Brush the mackerel with oil and make several diagonal slashes in the skin. Rub chopped herbs into the slashes and place on a grill pan. Grill them as you make the sauce, keeping an eagle eye out to see they don't burn (brush again with oil when they're flipped over).

Mix the egg yolks, mustard and herbs together in a pudding basin. Rest it in a saucepan above hot water and whisk for a minute or two until thoroughly blended. Then whisk in the butter, small bits at a time, until you have a sauce the consistency of mayonnaise. Take off the heat, add a good squeeze of lemon juice, pepper and salt.

Transfer the mackerel to hot plates and coat with a little of the sauce. Serve the rest separately.

Serves 4

● 10 minutes   ▣ 10 minutes   ✱

Grilled Mackerel with Rhubarb Purée

The success of this recipe depends on the rhubarb which must be ripe and very red, otherwise the colour will be disappointing.

4 fresh mackerel, cleaned and
  gutted

oil
watercress (optional)

Rhubarb Purée

1 lb (450g) ripe red rhubarb,
  trimmed and chopped
3–4 tablespoons sugar
2 small Cox's Orange Pippins,
  peeled and chopped

1/2 oz (15g) butter
juice of 1/2 small lemon
2 tablespoons port (optional)

Put the rhubarb and half the sugar into a heavy, medium saucepan. Cover with buttered paper and a lid and leave over moderate heat until the juices begin to run. Then add the apples, the butter and another tablespoon of sugar. Cover again with the buttered paper and continue cooking until the apples are just soft. Take off the heat and mash roughly until you have a thick, chunky purée. Add the lemon juice, port (if used) and more sugar if needed. Cover and chill until icy cold.* (Bring to room temperature before you grill the mackerel so the flavour of the purée has a chance to 'come to'.)

When ready to cook the mackerel, cut several diagonal slashes in the skin. Lightly oil the grill rack and place the fish on it. Brush the fish with oil and put under (but not too close) a hot grill. Grill on both sides until cooked through and the skin is crisp and nicely frizzled. Take out and serve at once with the rhubarb purée and fresh watercress if you have it.

Serves 4

● 15 minutes   ▣ 30 minutes   Chilling time: at least 1 hour   ◀ to *

Haddock with
Sesame Seed Crumbs

1 lb (450g) fresh haddock fillets	3 oz (75g) soft white breadcrumbs
1 oz (25g) butter	2 tablespoons sesame seeds
salt and pepper	1 tablespoon finely chopped fresh parsley
2 oz (50g) butter, melted	

Rinse the haddock fillets and wipe dry with kitchen paper. Lightly butter a shallow baking tin and arrange the fillets in it. Put knobs of the unmelted butter on each fillet and season well with salt and black pepper.

Mix the melted butter, breadcrumbs, sesame seeds and parsley together with a little salt and pepper. Scatter over the fish, covering them completely.* Bake in a preheated oven (350°F/Gas Mark 4/180°F), on the second shelf from the top, for 25–30 minutes or until the crumbs are golden brown. Take out and serve with sauté potatoes and a crisp vegetable.

Serves 2

 15 minutes ◉ 25 minutes ◐ to * ▲▲ ✦

Little Pots
of Smoked Haddock

1½ oz (40g) butter	1 lb (450g) smoked haddock fillets
10 oz (275g) button mushrooms, finely diced (except 4 large ones)	salt and pepper
2 level tablespoons flour	8 tablespoons dried brown breadcrumbs
½ pint (275ml) milk	1 oz (25g) butter
¼ pint (150ml) single cream	
1 tablespoon finely chopped parsley	

Melt the butter in a large, heavy saucepan. Add the diced mushrooms and cook for a few minutes until they have darkened. Lift them out carefully with a slotted spoon and put to one side. Add the flour to the pan and cook for a minute. Take off the heat and blend in the milk. Stir over moderate heat until the mixture thickens. Add the cream and parsley and blend well. Remove the skin from the haddock and flake into bite-size chunks. Add to the creamy sauce and heat gently for about 10 minutes. Season lightly with salt and pepper.

Divide the mixture between four large ramekins, 4 inches (10cm) in diameter. Quarter the remaining mushrooms and push four pieces down into each ramekin. Top with the breadcrumbs and knobs of the remaining butter.* Put to one side until needed or place straight away in a preheated oven (350°F/Gas Mark 4/180°F) and bake for 30–40 minutes or until bubbly and nicely browned. Serve with a crisp green salad, brown bread and butter.

Serves 4

 10 minutes ◉ 15 minutes + 35 minutes (oven) ◐ to * ▲▲

Cod with Garlic Mayonnaise

4 cod steaks or fillets

Garlic Mayonnaise

2 fat cloves of garlic, peeled	1 tablespoon white wine
salt	vinegar
2 large egg yolks	white pepper
1/2 pint olive or vegetable oil	

Put the cod into the oven (350°F/Gas Mark 4/180°C) to bake and as it cooks, prepare the aioli (garlic mayonnaise).

Crush the garlic cloves with a little salt in a mortar. Add the egg yolks and blend well, then whisk in the oil, drop by drop, as you would when making a mayonnaise. When it begins to thicken, pour the oil in a steady stream. Add the vinegar and season to taste with salt and white pepper. (Alternatively, this can all be done in a food processor: add the garlic cloves and whiz until finely chopped, then add the yolks with a little salt and then the oil, poured slowly through the top opening with the machine on. Blend in the vinegar and season to taste.)

Serve the cod fillets with a good dollop of aioli on the side and a spinach salad.

Serves 4

━ 10 minutes   ◙ 20–25 minutes   ✱

60

Cod with Cider and Mushrooms

4 cod steaks or fillets, about 1 lb (450g) total weight	1/2 lb (225g) button mushrooms, thickly sliced
1/4 pint (150ml) dry cider	2 level tablespoons flour
3 oz (75g) butter	juices from the fish made up to 1/2 pint (275ml) with chicken stock
salt and pepper	
1 small onion or 4 shallots, peeled and finely chopped	a little lemon juice (if needed)
1 small clove of garlic, crushed	chopped parsley
2 large carrots, peeled and cut into 2-inch (5cm) strips	

Arrange the cod in a buttered baking tin. Pour over the cider, dot with 1/2 oz (15g) butter and season with salt and pepper. Bake at 350°F/Gas Mark 4/180°C for 20 minutes or until the fish flakes easily with a fork. Lift out the fish (leaving any skin behind) with a fish slice and put on a plate. Pour the pan juices into a measuring jug.

As the fish cooks, melt 1 1/2 oz (40g) butter in a large, heavy saucepan and sauté the onion and garlic for 3–5 minutes. Add the carrots and mushrooms with a little salt and pepper. Cover with a buttered paper and lid and cook gently. When just tender, tip the vegetables and juices into a bowl.

Melt the remaining butter in the same pan and stir in the flour. Cook for a minute, then remove from the heat and gradually blend in the fish juices made up to 1/2 pint (275ml) with chicken stock. Stir over gentle heat until the mixture thickens. Simmer for several minutes, then return the vegetables and their juice to the pan. Flake the fish into medium chunks and add to the sauce. Season with salt, pepper and a little lemon juice if needed. Dust the top with parsley, then serve with boiled potatoes and cider.

Serves 4

━ 10 minutes   ◙ 20 minutes (oven) + 25–30 minutes   ◖

Monkfish with Bacon

Blindfolded, you might almost think this was scampi.

1 lb (450g) monkfish	1/2 lemon
4 rashers back bacon	chopped fresh parsley
12 button mushrooms	salt and black pepper
2 oz (50g) butter	

Carefully remove the central bone from the monkfish, then cut the flesh into large cubes. Cut each bacon rasher into three pieces.

Make the brochettes by threading first a mushroom, then a rolled-up piece of bacon, then a piece of fish on a skewer (you'll need four, about 7 inches/17.5cm long). Continue until the skewer is filled. Melt the butter in a shallow baking tin and tip half of it into a small cup. Arrange the brochettes in rows in the pan and turn them until completely coated in butter. Squeeze a little lemon juice and scatter chopped parsley over them, then season lightly with salt and freshly ground black pepper.* (They can be left like this – up to several hours – until needed.)

When ready to cook the brochettes, heat the grill. Place the baking tin with the fish about 2 inches (5cm) beneath it and grill each side until the bacon is very crisp. Brush each new side with melted butter and continue until all sides have been done. (Be careful not to overcook the fish – but it must be cooked through.) Take out, give another squeeze of lemon juice and light seasoning of salt and pepper. Arrange on a bed of hot rice, pour over the pan juices and serve.

Serves 2

🥘 10 minutes   ▣ 10 minutes   ◕ to *   ✴

Red Mullet with Fennel

Fennel seeds are found on the spice/herb racks of most supermarkets and delicatessens. They accentuate the flavour of the fennel bulb, and go well with cabbage.

2 good-sized red mullet, scaled but not gutted	1/2 teaspoon fennel seeds (optional)
1 1/2 oz (40g) butter	4 fl oz (100ml) chicken stock
1 medium onion, peeled and thinly sliced	1 tablespoon Pernod or brandy
1 large or 2 small fennel bulbs	salt and pepper

Rinse the mullet well under cold running water, then pat dry with kitchen paper.

Melt the butter in a heavy, medium saucepan and soften the onion in it until soft and transparent. Add the fennel and fennel seeds (if used) and toss well in the buttery juices. Pour in the chicken stock and cook, partly covered, over fairly high heat until the fennel is just tender. Blend in the Pernod or brandy and transfer with any juices in the pan to a large, lightly buttered gratin or ovenproof dish. Season lightly with salt and black pepper. Arrange the mullet on top, pressing them down into the fennel and onion bed. Season them with salt and pepper, then cover the dish with foil.* Put into a preheated oven (350°F/Gas Mark 4/180°C) and bake for about 20–30 minutes (this will depend on the size of the fish – be careful not to overcook them), basting occasionally. Take out and allow the dish to stand, covered, for 5 minutes. Then dish up on to hot plates and serve with boiled or mashed potatoes.

Serves 2

🥘 10 minutes   ▣ 15 minutes + 20 minutes (oven)   ◕ to *

61

Trout in a Paper Bag

2 oz (50g) butter
1 small onion or 4 shallots,
    peeled and finely chopped
1 clove of garlic, crushed
$^{1}/_{2}$ lb (225g) button
    mushrooms, diced

$^{1}/_{2}$ lb (225g) baby courgettes,
    diced
salt and pepper
4 small trout, cleaned and
    gutted

Start by melting $^{1}/_{2}$ oz (25g) butter in a large, heavy saucepan and cook the onion until soft and transparent. Add the remaining butter to the pan with the garlic, mushrooms and courgettes. Toss until well coated in the buttery juices, then add a good seasoning of salt and pepper. Cover with a buttered paper and a lid and cook over gentle heat for 10–15 minutes.

Cut out four large heart-shapes in foil or greaseproof paper. Open them out flat and brush the inside lightly with oil. Rinse the trout well under cold running water, then pat dry with kitchen paper. Put one in the centre of one half of each heart and season well with salt and pepper. Cover each one with a generous dollop of the mushroom mixture and its juices, spreading it down the length of the fish. Fold over the paper or foil to enclose the fish completely, pinch the edges together and crimp tightly. Transfer to a baking tray* and place in a preheated oven (350°F/Gas Mark 4/180°F) for 20–30 minutes (depending on size of the fish). Take out and slide each parcel on to a hot plate. Take to the table, cut a cross in each one and peel back the paper. Eat straight from the bag.

Serves 4

🥄 15 minutes ▣ 15 minutes + 25 minutes (oven) ◖ to *

62

Moules Marinière

4 pints (2.25 litres) fresh
    mussels
1 tablespoon butter
3 shallots, peeled and finely
    chopped
$^{1}/_{2}$ pint (275ml) dry white
    wine
2–3 tablespoons finely
    chopped parsley

1 sprig fresh thyme
scrap of bay leaf
a little pepper
beurre manié made with 1
    tablespoon soft butter and
    $^{1}/_{2}$ tablespoon flour

Scrub the mussels well, removing the beard and discarding any which are cracked or which feel abnormally light or heavy. Keep in a bowl of cold water until needed.

Melt the butter in a large, deep saucepan (ideally a sauté pan with a lid). Cook the shallots in the butter until soft, then add the wine, herbs, a little black pepper and mussels. Bring up to the boil, cover and cook quickly – shaking the pan occasionally – for a few minutes until the mussels have opened. Lift them out with a slotted spoon and keep warm in a heated dish (Discard any mussels which haven't opened.)

Rapidly boil the mussel liquid until reduced by half, then add the *beurre manié*, bit by bit, until the sauce has thickened. Taste and adjust the seasoning if necessary. Divide the mussels between heated plates, pour over the sauce and serve with lots of crusty bread and unsalted butter.

Serves 2

🥄 15 minutes ▣ 10 minutes

Atlantic Gratinée

1½ lbs (675g) haddock fillets
¼ pint (150ml) dry white wine
2 fl oz (50ml) water
sprig of parsley, few slices
   onion, few peppercorns

1 oz (25g) butter
salt and pepper
¼ lb (100g) cooked peeled
   prawns

Sauce

1½ oz (40g) butter
8 spring onions, finely chopped
2 large stalks celery, finely
   diced
1 oz (25g) flour

juices from the fish made up to
   ½ pint (275ml) milk
1 tablespoon finely chopped
   parsley
2 oz (50g) Cheddar, grated

Rinse and dry the fillets and arrange in a shallow baking tin. Pour over the wine and water and scatter a sprig of parsley, a few onion slices and peppercorns on top. Dot with the butter and season well with salt and pepper. Cook in a moderate oven (350°F/Gas Mark 4/180°C) for 20–25 minutes, or until the fish is opaque and flakes easily with a fork. Lift the fish out and strain the pan juices into a jug.

Meanwhile soften the onions and celery in 1 oz (25g) butter, then cover with buttered paper and cook over a very low heat until the fish is ready. Then add the remaining butter and stir in the flour. Cook for a minute, then remove from the heat and gradually blend in the fish juices mixed with the milk. Stir over a moderate heat until it comes to the boil and thickens. Simmer for several minutes, then add the parsley and Cheddar (without boiling). Season to taste.

Arrange the haddock fillets in diagonal rows in a large, buttered gratin dish. Scatter the prawns in rows between them. Season lightly, then pour over the sauce.* Place under a hot grill (or in a hot oven if prepared ahead) until bubbly.

Serves 4–6

◗ 10 minutes   ◖ 45 minutes   ◗ to *

Prawns with Lemon and Garlic

1 lb (450g) fresh cooked
   prawns in their shells
¼ pint (150ml) dry white
   wine

2 oz (50g) butter
a little finely chopped parsley
good squeeze of lemon juice
black pepper

Rinse the prawns well under cold running water, removing their egg sacs but not their shells or heads. Drain, then dry well in a clean tea towel.

Pour the white wine into a large, heavy sauté or frying pan. Boil rapidly until reduced by half then add the butter and lower the heat slightly. Add the prawns to the pan (you may have to do this in two lots – if so, hold back half the wine and butter) with a little chopped parsley and lemon juice. Cook, shaking the pan frequently, until they are lightly 'glazed' on each side (this will take about 5–8 minutes). Give a further squeeze of lemon juice and add a little black pepper, then tip the prawns on to individual plates with the pan juices. Serve at once with lots of granary bread and butter.

Serves 2

◗ 10 minutes   ◖ about 10 minutes   ✱

Kippers with Scrambled Egg

4 large soft white rolls
2 oz (50g) butter
2 large kipper fillets (¹/₂ lb/225g total weight)
dash of lemon juice
6 large eggs
splash of water

black pepper
¹/₂ bunch of watercress, top leaves shredded
1 tablespoon double cream or top of the milk
¹/₂ bunch of watercress, unshredded

Cut large circles from the top of the rolls. Pull out most of the bread inside to leave a large hollow for the eggs and from the inside of the lid so that it will sit flat. Put ¹/₂ oz (15g) of butter in each one, cover with their lids and wrap in foil (or put into a brown paper bag and dampen the top with water). Put the rolls into a hot oven while you prepare the kippers and eggs.

Grill the kippers, then drain well on kitchen paper. Remove the skin, any random bones and flake into fairly good-sized pieces. Add a dash of lemon juice and put to one side. Melt the remaining butter in a large, heavy saucepan. Whisk the eggs lightly with a splash of water and freshly ground pepper. Scrape them into the pan and cook until they are just beginning to set. Remove from the heat, add the kipper chunks, shredded watercress and cream, then return to a gentle heat. Cook briefly – only until the eggs have become creamy. Remove from the heat immediately and take the rolls out of the oven. Place on individual plates and fill the rolls with the scrambled egg, piling it up at the top. Put the lids on at an angle and serve with sprigs of watercress.

Serves 4

━ 10 minutes ◉ about 10 minutes

64

Salmon Kedgeree

1 15-oz (425g) tin red or pink salmon
10 oz (275g) long-grain rice, uncooked
2 oz (50g) butter
6 oz (175g) finely chopped onion
¹/₂ lb (225g) finely sliced button mushrooms
5 level tablespoons flour

¹/₂ level teaspoon mild curry powder
1 pint (575ml) milk
1 teaspoon lemon juice
2 rounded tablespoons finely chopped parsley
salt and pepper
3 large hard-boiled eggs
watercress or chopped parsley

Drain the juices from the salmon and reserve. Remove the skin and any bones and break into medium chunks. Put the rice on and cook in your usual way.

Meanwhile, make the sauce: melt half the butter in a large saucepan or deep skillet. Add the onion and cook until soft. Add the remaining butter with the mushrooms and cook for several minutes. Stir in the flour and curry powder and cook for a minute. Take the pan off the heat and gradually blend in the milk. Return to moderate heat and stir until it comes to the boil. Add the lemon juice, the salmon juices and parsley, then season to taste with salt and pepper. Simmer gently for 5–10 minutes, until nicely thickened. Then fold in the salmon chunks and the eggs, cut into quarters lengthwise. Taste and adjust the seasoning if necessary.

Put the hot rice on to a large, hot serving platter. Pile it round the sides, leaving a hollow in the middle. Pour the sauce in the centre, garnish with watercress and serve.

Serves 6

━ 10 minutes ◉ 25 minutes sauce only

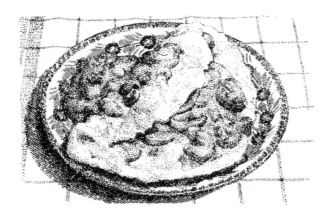

Eggs

One of the simplest, best suppers is an omelette. All it requires is practice. The only essential equipment is a small, heavy pan (7 inches/17.5cm in diameter for a 2–3 egg omelette) with a flat bottom and rounded sides. Before the butter is added, the pan should be so hot that a drop of water evaporates almost immediately. Speed is crucial and the whole operation should take barely two minutes from the moment the eggs hit the pan to the second they slip, perfectly rounded, on to a hot plate.

Thus, the ideal candidate for a quick supper. Plump it up, if you like, with a few juicy morsels: cooked chicken livers or shredded ham, mushrooms, tomatoes, cheese, prawns or sautéed spring onions. The simplest and perhaps the best is an omelette *aux fines herbes*, when finely chopped fresh parsley, chives, chervil, tarragon (any of these) are added to the eggs with a few knobs of butter.

The mystique which surrounds the soufflé bears no relation to its humble ingredients. Nor to its manufacture which requires only a good recipe and no distractions. Concentration is the one essential, for a heavy hand with the flour or over-whisked egg whites will result in thick gunge. The size of the dish is equally important. A 4- or 5-egg soufflé should be baked in a round soufflé dish, 7 inches (17.5cm) in diameter and 3$^{1}/_{2}$ inches (8.5cm) deep. If the dish is too large, the soufflé will never see the light of day; if too small, it will balloon up and *over* the sides of the dish.

The cheese base for the soufflé can be made ahead but must be warmed up slightly before the whisked egg whites are folded in (otherwise the effort of being folded into a stiff mixture will break down the whites irrevocably). Though it may sound hopelessly anachronistic, it *does* make a difference if the egg whites are whisked by hand. You get almost twice the volume and don't run the same risk of over-beating as you do with an electric whisk. (If you're in a great rush, whisk them electrically to the soft peak stage, then whisk by hand until stiff.)

Individual soufflés make a stylish supper. Use large ramekins (4 inches/10cm in diameter) and bake them in a roasting tin half-filled with warm water (this ensures height without the mixture drying out). Courgette, spinach and stilton are all successful when done in individual dishes. If you want to prepare them ahead, borrow a trick from the Dorchester. Fill the soufflé dishes two-thirds full and put straight into the freezer. When ready to cook, take the dishes out of the freezer and put into a preheated oven (400°F/Gas Mark 6/200°C). Thirty minutes later – voilà, les soufflés!

The Perfect Cheese Soufflé

2 oz (50g) butter
1¹/₂ oz (40g) plain flour
¹/₂ teaspoon Dijon mustard
¹/₂ pint (275ml) milk
4 oz (100g) grated cheese
  (Cheddar, Gruyère,
  Parmesan or any two of
  these)

salt and pepper
pinch of cayenne pepper
4 large egg yolks
5 large egg whites

Preheat the oven to 400°F/Gas Mark 6/200°C. Grease a soufflé dish 7 inches (17.5cm) in diameter and 3¹/₂ inches (8.5cm) deep. Melt the butter in a large, heavy-based saucepan. Stir in the flour and cook for 1 minute, then add the mustard and cook for a minute longer. Take off the heat and gradually blend in the milk. Return to the heat and stir until the mixture comes to the boil. Add the cheese and stir until thoroughly blended (being careful not to let it boil). Season to taste with salt, pepper and cayenne pepper. Take off the heat and whisk in the egg yolks, one at a time.*

Put the egg whites into a large, spotlessly clean bowl. Add a pinch of salt to them, then whisk until stiff. Using a rubber spatula, scrape the yolk mixture out of the pan and down one side of the bowl the whites are in. Carefully fold the whites into the yolk mixture, then tip it all into the prepared dish. Put straight into the preheated oven (in the centre) and reduce the temperature to 375°F/Gas Mark 5/190°C. Bake for 40–45 minutes or until well risen and golden (don't peek until at least 30 minutes have elapsed). Take out and serve at once.

Serves 4

🥄 10–15 minutes   ⊡ 10 minutes + 45 minutes (oven)
◒ to * then reheat to lukewarm

Spinach Soufflé

¹/₂ lb (225g) cooked fresh
  spinach or frozen chopped
  spinach
salt and pepper
freshly grated nutmeg
2 oz (50g) butter
4 oz (100g) onion, peeled

1¹/₂ oz (40g) plain flour
¹/₂ pint (275ml) milk
2 oz (50g) good Cheddar,
  grated
3 large eggs, separated
2 tablespoons grated
  Parmesan (optional)

Preheat the oven to 375°F/Gas Mark 5/190°C. Generously butter 4 large ramekins, 4 inches (10cm) in diameter, or 1 small soufflé dish.

Chop the spinach finely and cook until quite dry, stirring occasionally. (If using frozen spinach: thaw completely, tip off excess water, then cook as above.) Season well with salt, pepper and nutmeg.

Chop the onion *very* finely and sauté in half the butter until soft. Add the remaining butter and tip in the flour. Cook for 1–2 minutes, then remove from the heat and blend in the milk. Cook gently until it thickens. Whisk in the spinach, then the Cheddar (without boiling). Season to taste with salt, pepper and more nutmeg if needed. Cool slightly, then whisk in the egg yolks one at a time.*

Place in the middle of the oven a roasting tin containing enough water to come halfway up the ramekins. Whisk the whites with a pinch of salt until stiff. Blend a tablespoonful of them into the spinach mixture to loosen it, then fold in the remaining whites. Fill the ramekins to the top, then level off and place in the waiting tin. Bake for 20–25 minutes or until well risen. Take out, dust with Parmesan and serve.

Serves 4

🥄 15 minutes   ⊡ 20 minutes + 25 minutes (oven)
◒ to * then reheat to lukewarm

The Two Sisters' Soufflé

Though not a true soufflé, this delicate puff of cheese and egg is invaluable as a do-ahead dish. (The two sisters are my youthful aunts who manage to cook superbly and do twenty other things at the same time.)

6 thin slices of a large white sandwich loaf (homemade or bakery – not a sponge rubber one)
6 oz (175g) medium-strong farmhouse Cheddar, finely grated
1 large spring onion, chopped

2 large eggs, lightly beaten
1/4 teaspoon dry English mustard
good pinch cayenne pepper
1/4 teaspoon salt
lots of ground black pepper
11 fl oz (300ml) milk
1 oz (25g) melted butter

Trim the crusts from the bread slices and cut into fingers. Generously butter a soufflé dish (7 inches/17.5cm × 2½ inches/6cm is ideal) and in it put layers of the bread fingers and cheese, with a scattering of chopped spring onion in between (ending with a layer of cheese).

Beat the eggs lightly in a bowl, then whisk in the mustard, cayenne pepper, salt, black pepper, milk and melted butter. Pour slowly into the dish (letting it sink to the bottom layers before you pour more in – otherwise it will overflow) until it is all in. Cover with cling-film and leave for several hours (or overnight in a refrigerator).* Bring to room temperature and bake in a preheated oven (350°F/Gas Mark 4/180°C) for an hour or until well risen and a deep golden brown. Take out and serve at once with a crisp green salad.

Serves 4

◗ 10 minutes Soaking time: 3–12 hours ◉ 1 hour (oven) ◗ to *

Pipérade

A rosy blend of tomatoes and egg that would brighten up any grey evening.

1 oz (25g) butter
2 rashers back bacon, finely chopped
1 medium onion, peeled and thinly sliced
1 small red or green pepper, thinly sliced

1/2 clove of garlic, crushed
1 lb (450g) ripe tomatoes, roughly chopped
salt and pepper
6 large eggs
chopped chervil or parsley

Melt the butter in a heavy, medium saucepan and add the bacon. Cook until the fat begins to run, then add the onion, red or green pepper and garlic. Cook slowly, stirring occasionally, until the onion is golden. Add the tomatoes and their juices and continue cooking for about 20 minutes or until reduced to a thick purée. Season well with salt and black pepper.

Beat the eggs lightly with a splash of water and light seasoning of salt and pepper. Tip into the pan and cook over moderate heat, stirring as little as possible, until they have the consistency of rather moist scrambled eggs. Check the seasoning, give a light dusting of parsley or chervil and serve at once.

Serves 4

◗ 10 minutes ◉ 35 minutes ✱

Mumbled Eggs

In the last century, this little dish became de rigeur at fashionable luncheons and ball suppers. The eggs were dished up on hot muffins spread first with a layer of caviar.

4 muffins (English, not American)
3 oz (75g) butter
4 rashers back bacon, cut into small dice
1/2 lb (225g) button mushrooms, thinly sliced
salt and pepper
6 large eggs
splash of water
4–6 tablespoons double cream
chopped parsley or chervil (dried or fresh)

Toast the muffins on each side, then split and butter (using 1 oz/25g). Put them on individual plates (2 halves per plate) and keep warm.

Melt another ounce (25g) of butter in a small frying pan and add the bacon. Cook until just crisp, then add the mushrooms. Stir until well coated in the buttery juices, then cook for several minutes. Season lightly with salt and pepper, then keep warm.

In a medium-heavy saucepan, melt the remaining butter. Beat the eggs lightly with a splash of water and seasoning of salt and pepper. Pour into the pan and stir over a low heat until they show signs of setting. Pour in the cream and continue stirring until the eggs begin to set again. Then take off the heat and add *half* the bacon/mushroom mixture. Give one quick stir (no more or the texture of the eggs will be spoiled) and divide the eggs among the muffin halves. Top with the remaining mushrooms, bacon and light dusting of parsley. Serve at once.

Serves 4

🍴 10 minutes   ◉ 15 minutes   ✱

68

Baked Eggs Savoyarde

A Sunday supper which no one seems to tire of.

3/4 lb (350g) new potatoes, well scrubbed
2 oz (50g) butter
1 medium onion, peeled and thinly sliced
4 rashers back bacon, cut into strips
2–3 tablespoons vegetable oil
4 large eggs
salt and pepper
4 tablespoons double cream
1 tablespoon finely chopped parsley
2 tablespoons grated Parmesan or Cheddar

Boil the potatoes until just tender, then drain well. Melt half the butter in a heavy, medium saucepan or frying pan. Add the onion and cook until golden, then add the bacon and cook until crisp. Lift both out with a slotted spoon and put to one side. Add 2 tablespoons of oil to the pan with the remaining butter and, when hot, add the potatoes cut in thick slices. Fry until golden on both sides, adding more oil as needed.

Mix the onions, bacon and potatoes in the bottom of a buttered gratin dish, then spread out to make an even layer. Carefully crack the eggs on to the mixture, keeping them well apart. Season well with salt and pepper, then pour the cream over evenly. Scatter the parsley and cheese over the top. Put the dish into a preheated oven (400°F/Gas Mark 6/200°C) and bake for 15–20 minutes or until the eggs have set. Take out and serve with crusty bread and unsalted butter.

Serves 4

🍴 10 minutes   ◉ 30 minutes + 20 minutes (oven)

Molly-coddled Eggs with Leeks

1½ lbs (675g) leeks
1½ oz (40g) butter
salt and black pepper
½ bunch of watercress,
   rinsed, dried and shredded
2–3 tablespoons thick cream
4 large eggs, at room
   temperature
1–2 tablespoons grated
   Parmesan cheese

Top and tail the leeks, then halve lengthwise and clean thoroughly. Cut into ½-inch (1cm) chunks. Melt the butter in a medium, heavy saucepan and, when foaming, add the leeks. Toss until well coated with the buttery juices, then cover with a buttered paper and a lid. Cook for 10–15 minutes (the leeks should be soft but not mushy). Season well with salt and freshly ground black pepper, then mix in the watercress and cream. Put to one side.

Bring a saucepan of water to the boil and carefully lower the eggs into it. Bring back to the boil and boil for 5 minutes exactly. Drain off the water, replace with cold water and, when cool enough to handle, peel under cold running water. Divide half the leek mixture among four ramekins or spread out in a small gratin dish. Bury the eggs in the leeks and top with the remaining leeks (it doesn't matter if the eggs are not completely covered). Scatter the Parmesan on top and put to one side until needed. When ready to bake, cover the dish (or ramekins) with foil* and put into a preheated oven (350°F/Gas Mark 4/180°C) for 20–30 minutes or until piping hot. Serve with brown bread and butter.

Serves 2

  5 minutes   ◨10–15 minutes + 25 minutes (oven)   ◕ to *

SC - E✹

Eggs in Bathrobes

4 large granary rolls
1 oz (25g) melted butter
4 oz (100g) finely chopped
   onion
2½ oz (65g) butter
½ lb (225g) button
   mushrooms, finely diced
1 oz (25g) flour
¾ pint (425ml) milk
½ bunch of watercress,
   shredded
salt and pepper
4 poached eggs
2 oz (50g) grated Cheddar or
   Gruyère cheese

Cut a large circle from the top of the rolls and pull out most of the bread inside, leaving a deep 'nest' for the eggs. Brush the interior with melted butter. Then put on a baking tray in a moderately hot oven for 20 minutes or until crisp.

As they bake, prepare the sauce. Sauté the onion in 1½ oz (40g) butter until almost golden. Add the mushrooms and cook for several minutes. Lift both out of the pan and put to one side. Add the remaining butter to the pan and stir in the flour. Cook for a minute, then take off the heat and gradually blend in the milk. Stir over moderate heat until it boils. Simmer for several minutes, then stir in the mushroom/onion mixture with their juices and the watercress. Season well with salt and pepper.

Put the rolls in a shallow baking tin or gratin dish. Place a poached egg in each roll and cover with the sauce (it should flow over each roll, so set them slightly apart). Scatter the grated cheese on top and put under the grill for a few minutes until bubbling and hot.

Serves 4

  10–15 minutes   ◨ 25 minutes   ✱

Ambushed Eggs

First catch your egg . . .

1 8-oz (225g) packet frozen
   leaf spinach, thawed
salt and pepper
grated nutmeg
1 oz (25g) butter
2 level tablespoons flour
12 fl oz (350ml) milk
sprig of parsley, and slice of
   onion

1 tablespoon grated Parmesan
2 oz (50g) good Cheddar,
   grated
4 large eggs
2 slices cooked ham, shredded
2 tablespoons dried wholemeal
   breadcrumbs

Put the spinach into a saucepan and cook uncovered until dry. Season with salt, pepper and a little grated nutmeg, then put to one side.

Melt the butter in a medium saucepan and stir in the flour. Cook for a minute, then take off the heat and gradually blend in the hot milk. Add the onion and parsley, then stir over low heat until the mixture thickens. Simmer gently for several minutes, then scoop out the onion and parsley. Add the Parmesan and Cheddar with a good seasoning of salt and pepper. Stir until the cheese has melted, then put to one side.

Poach the eggs and drain on kitchen paper. Divide the spinach between two small ovenproof dishes (the ones with 'ears' are perfect) or put it all in a small gratin dish. Place the poached eggs on top and scatter the ham strips over them. Pour over the cheese sauce and top with the breadcrumbs. Put the dish into a hot oven or under the grill until bubbling and lightly browned. Serve at once.

Serves 2

🥄 15 minutes   ◉ 35 minutes

70

Eggs Benedicta

This is Eggs Benedict for the figure-conscious. The calorie-laden butter is partly replaced by the virtuous yogurt.

2 large egg yolks
good squeeze of lemon juice
1 teaspoon pale French
   mustard
2 oz (50g) unsalted butter
5 oz (150ml) natural yogurt
2 teaspoons white wine
   vinegar

salt and white pepper
2 English muffins, halved
4 small slices cooked ham
4 large eggs
chopped parsley, tarragon or
   chives

Put the egg yolks, lemon juice and mustard into a small Pyrex bowl. Set over a pan of gently simmering water. Whisk until well blended, then whisk in the butter bit by bit. When thick and mousse-like, whisk in the yogurt. Keep over the same heat, whisking from time to time for 5–10 minutes, until the mixture thickens again. Then add the vinegar and season to taste. Take the pan off the heat and leave the bowl (covered) over the hot water. (This sauce can be made the day ahead, then reheated. After making it, dot the surface with small knobs of butter and cover the bowl with cling-film. If it seems too thick when you need it, whisk in a little boiling water.)

Toast and butter the muffin halves and keep warm in the oven. Cut the ham to fit the muffins and put to one side. Poach the eggs, lift out and drain. Put one muffin half on each plate. Top with a slice of ham and poached egg. Pour over just enough of the yogurt sauce to cover them and scatter chopped herbs on top.

Serves 4, or 2 ravenous eaters

🥄 10 minutes   ◉ 25 minutes   ✱

Spanish Tortilla

Banish the thought of leaden tortillas – this one is slim and light. Any left over is delicious cold.

1¹/₂ oz (40g) butter
1–2 tablespoons olive or vegetable oil
2 oz (50g) back bacon, finely diced
3 oz (75g) finely chopped onion
¹/₂ green pepper, chopped
6 small new potatoes, cooked, *or* 1 medium cooked potato, peeled
4 oz (100g) cooked or tinned *petits pois* (failing those, ordinary peas)
6 large eggs
salt and pepper

Heat 1 oz (25g) of butter and 1 tablespoon of the oil in a large, heavy skillet (10 inches/25cm is perfect). When hot, add the bacon dice, onion and pepper. Cook until the bacon is crisp and the onion golden. Cut the potatoes into thick slices and add to the pan (with more oil if you need it). Cook until they are nicely browned on both sides, then add the drained peas.

Whisk the eggs briefly with a splash of water and good seasoning of salt and pepper. Add the remaining butter to the pan and when hot, pour in the eggs. Cook as you would an omelette, lifting the edges so that the uncooked egg can run underneath. When the bottom seems to be lightly browned and there is only a thin layer of uncooked egg on top, take the pan off the heat and put it 3 or 4 inches (7.5 or 10cm) under a hot grill. Leave for several minutes until the top is just barely set (don't leave it too long or you'll end up with rubber). Cut into wedges and lift out with a fish slice.

Serves 4

◖ 10 minutes   ◉ 20 minutes   ✱

Omelette Arnold Bennett

Arnold Bennett ordered this omelette so often at the Savoy that in the end they named it after him.

¹/₂ lb (225g) smoked haddock fillets
2 oz (50g) butter
6 large eggs
salt and freshly ground black pepper
2 fl oz (50ml) double cream
2 tablespoons freshly grated Parmesan cheese
chopped parsley or chervil

Flake the haddock into medium chunks, removing any skin and bones. Melt half the butter in a small saucepan and add the fish. Warm over very low heat until piping hot, then cover and keep warm until the eggs are ready.

Crack the eggs into a bowl, add 2 teaspoons of water and a good seasoning of salt and pepper. Beat lightly with a fork until well blended. Melt the remaining butter in a large, heavy frying pan (or two small ones) over moderately high heat. When the butter is foamy, pour in the eggs. When the base of the omelette has set, scatter the haddock evenly over the top. A few seconds later, pour the cream and cheese over. Cook for several seconds longer, then put the pan under a hot grill and leave for barely a minute, until the outside edge of the omelette is a light golden brown. Cut at once into pie-shaped wedges (if using two small pans, cut in half) and transfer to heated plates. Dust the top lightly with parsley and serve.

Serves 4

◖ 10 minutes   ◉ 10 minutes   ✱

Omelette Bonne Femme

1½ oz (40g) butter
1 small onion, peeled and
  thinly sliced
2 rashers back bacon, diced

5 large eggs
salt and pepper
chopped herbs

Take ½ oz (15g) of the butter and heat it in a small saucepan. Sauté the onion and bacon in it until the onion is golden. Keep over a low heat until needed.

Break the eggs into a bowl and whisk until well blended with a little water, salt and pepper. Melt half the remaining butter in a small, heavy pan (about 7 inches/17.5cm in diameter) and, when very hot, pour in half the eggs. Shake the pan until it shows signs of setting. Then lift the edges, allowing the uncooked egg to run underneath. Scatter half the onion and bacon mixture on top with a few chopped herbs, cook briefly, then fold the omelette over and tip on to a hot plate. Repeat for the second omelette.

Serves 2

🍮 5 minutes   ◉ 10 minutes   ✹

72

Soufflé Omelette

For a sweet version, add a teaspoon of sugar to the eggs and a little cooked apple just before folding, then dust the top with icing sugar.

3 large eggs
a little water
chopped fresh herbs (tarragon,
  chives, parsley)

salt and pepper
1 oz (25g) butter
a little grated Parmesan or
  Cheddar

Separate the eggs, putting the whites into a large, spotlessly clean bowl. Beat the yolks lightly with a splash of water, add the chopped herbs and a good seasoning of salt and pepper.

Put a small, heavy pan, about 7 inches (17.5cm) in diameter, over a moderately high heat. Add a pinch of salt to the egg whites and whisk until stiff. Scrape the yolks into the whites with a spatula and fold in lightly. Add half the butter to the pan and when it stops foaming, pour in half the eggs. Proceed as you would with an ordinary omelette, pushing the frothy egg to the sides and then lifting them, so it can flow underneath. Shake the pan frequently to prevent sticking and when the bottom is a rich golden brown, scatter half the cheese over the top. Fold the omelette in half and carefully flip on to a warm plate. Repeat for the second omelette, then eat at once.

Serves 2

🍮 5 minutes   ◉ 6 minutes   ✹

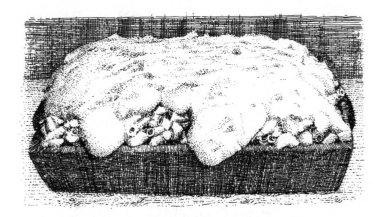

Pasta and Rice

A first visit to Italy reveals that all pasta is not spaghetti, it does not always come bathed in bolognese sauce and, furthermore, it is *chewy*.

Fresh pasta is so dramatically better than the dried that it is worth the search to find it. Marks and Spencer, large supermarkets and most delicatessens now stock it. Fresh pasta will take far less time to cook than the dried variety so watch it like a hawk. The thinnest types need only a minute in boiling water (including the time it takes to come back to the boil).

Preparing pasta is easy once you've found a pot large enough to cook it in. Fill with water, cover and bring to a rolling boil. Add a good tablespoon of salt and tip in the pasta. Stir briefly with a wooden fork and quickly return the water to the boil. Dried pasta will take three to six minutes to cook, depending on its thickness. Take the pot off the heat to test a strand and, if *al dente*, drain immediately in a large colander. Shake it vigorously to get rid of excess water (leaving just a little to prevent sticking) and transfer to a hot serving dish. Season well, add the sauce and serve *pronto*.

The string pastas – linguine, tagliatelle, spaghetti – all combine well with cream sauces. The shapes – particularly tubes and shells – are ideal for sauces with 'bits' (mushrooms, aubergine, sausage, seafood) as they trap the filling and make succulent mouthfuls. Wholewheat and buckwheat pasta, with their slight nuttiness, go well with a creamy or very savoury sauce.

Stock up on freshly grated Parmesan cheese so that you never have to resort to the packet variety – which is dry, strong and bitter. Alternatively, buy a wedge of Parmesan and grate it as needed. (Though it may seem expensive at the time, it will keep for months and is cheaper in the long run.)

Rice ranks with pasta as being one of the easiest and cheapest ways of producing a quick meal. A spiced pilau takes no more than twenty minutes to make and provides a superb partner for lamb or chicken. With the addition of vegetables, prawns, meat or chicken, it makes a filling meal in itself. Wholegrain rice – a blend of white long-grain and wild rice – is now widely available and well worth trying. The round-grain *arborio* rice is used for Italian risottos, where the liquid is stirred in, small amounts at a time, to make a rich, creamy mass. Leftover rice can be used for vegetable fried rice, a *tian* of carrots or as a stuffing for tomatoes, peppers, aubergines or courgettes.

Tagliatelle with Mushrooms, Bacon and Garlic

1 lb (450g) fresh tagliatelle or linguine *or* ³/₄ lb (350g) dried

salt and black pepper
grated Parmesan cheese
chopped parsley or herbs

Sauce
1¹/₂ oz (40g) butter
4 rashers back bacon, cut into thin strips
2 large cloves of garlic, crushed

¹/₂ lb (225g) button mushrooms, finely diced
3 fl oz (75ml) dry white wine

Fill a large pot with water, cover and bring up to the boil.

As you wait for the water to boil, begin the sauce. Melt half the butter in a heavy, medium saucepan or frying pan and add the bacon and garlic. Cook over moderate heat, stirring from time to time, until the bacon is almost crisp. Add the mushrooms and the remaining butter to the pan and continue cooking until the mushrooms have softened and darkened in colour. Pour in the wine and leave until it has reduced by about a third. Keep the pan over a very low heat (covered) until the pasta is ready.

When the water has come to a rolling boil, throw in a handful of salt and the pasta. Stir once with a wooden fork then bring back to the boil and cook (uncovered) for about a minute (if using fresh pasta) or 3–5 minutes (if using dried). Tip the pasta into a large colander, drain well, then put into a heated serving dish. Season well with salt and pepper. Pour the sauce over, then scatter a little Parmesan cheese and chopped herbs on top. Take to the table, toss and eat.

Serves 4

◗ 10 minutes   ◉ 15 minutes   ◖ sauce only   ✳

74

Pasta with Blue Cheese and Toasted Walnuts

2 oz (50g) shelled walnut halves or pieces
8 oz (225g) fresh tagliatelle or linguine, half white, half

green *or* 6 oz (175g) dried
chopped chervil (dried or fresh)

Blue Cheese Sauce
1 oz (25g) butter
¹/₄ pint (150ml) double cream
3 oz (75g) ripe German Blue Brie or a mild Gorgonzola, rind removed

generous dash of dry white wine (optional)
salt and white pepper

Put the walnuts into a shallow baking tin and then into a moderately hot oven. Leave until crisp and nicely browned, then chop roughly and keep warm.

As the walnuts toast, begin the sauce. Melt the butter in a small, heavy saucepan and blend in the cream. Break the blue cheese into small pieces, then whisk gradually into the sauce. Simmer gently, whisking all the time, until smooth. Add a little white wine and season with salt and pepper. Put to one side, then reheat gently as the pasta cooks.

Bring a large pot of water to a rolling boil, add a good tablespoonful of salt and then the pasta. Stir once as it comes back to the boil and cook uncovered until *al dente*. Drain well, then divide the pasta between hot plates. Season with salt and black pepper, then put a generous dollop of sauce in the middle of each bed of pasta. Scatter chopped walnuts and chervil on top and serve at once.

Serves 2

◗ 5 minutes   ◉ 15 minutes + 20 minutes (oven)   ✳

Fettucine with Peas and Ham

Fettucine, Rome's own brand of tagliatelle, is of shoelace width and particularly suited to sauces with cream.

¹/₂ lb (225g) green fettucine or tagliatelle, freshly made if possible	salt grated Parmesan cheese

Sauce

1¹/₂ oz (40g) butter	¹/₂ level teaspoon good meat glaze or Bovril
2 shallots or button onions, peeled and finely chopped	8 fl oz (225ml) double cream
2 oz (50g) roast or smoked ham, finely shredded	salt and black pepper
4 oz (100g) *petits pois*, drained of juice	

Start by making the sauce. Melt the butter in a heavy pan and add the shallots. Cook gently until golden. Add the ham and cook for several minutes, stirring occasionally. Stir in the peas, meat glaze and cream and simmer very gently for 2–3 minutes, until slightly thickened. Season with salt and freshly ground black pepper and keep warm until the pasta is ready.

Bring a large pot of water to the boil, add a tablespoon of salt and then the pasta. Stir well with a wooden fork or spoon and cook uncovered until *al dente* (if using fresh pasta, this will take barely a minute). Drain the pasta well, then tip into a hot serving dish. Season with salt and black pepper. Make sure the sauce is very hot, then pour over the pasta. Take to the table immediately and serve with grated Parmesan.

Serves 2

🍲 5 minutes   ◉ 15 minutes   ✱

Tortellini with Creamy Tomato Sauce

Tortellini are round and ring-shaped, frequently made with spinach-flavoured pasta. (Tortelloni are flat squares of filled pasta.)

1 lb (450g) tortellini (preferably green)	grated Parmesan cheese

Creamy Tomato Sauce

2 oz (50g) butter	salt and pepper
6 oz (175g) finely chopped onion	pinch of sugar
1 large carrot, peeled and finely diced	1 teaspoon finely chopped basil (preferably fresh)
1 14-oz (400g) tin Italian tomatoes	4 fl oz (100ml) double cream

Heat the butter in a large skillet and, when hot, add the onion and carrot. Sauté slowly, stirring occasionally, until the onion is golden. Add the tomatoes and their juice, breaking them up with a wooden spoon. Add a good seasoning of salt and pepper, then a pinch of sugar and the basil. Simmer uncovered for 15–20 minutes, until it is thick but not dry. Stir in the cream and heat gently until very hot again. Adjust the seasoning if necessary. Liquidize if you like a smooth sauce – otherwise, leave as is* – and keep warm.

Add a good tablespoonful of salt to a large pot of boiling water and add the tortellini. Stir until it returns to the boil, then boil uncovered for 8–10 minutes or until the pasta is *al dente*. Drain well, then transfer immediately to a hot serving dish. Pour the sauce on top and serve at once with grated Parmesan.

Serves 4

🍲 5 minutes   ◉ about 40 minutes   ◒ to *

Spaghetti for Crowds

2 lbs (900g) spaghetti   salt

Sausage and Tomato Sauce

2 tablespoons olive oil	1 teaspoon brown sugar
4 oz (100g) finely chopped onion	1 teaspoon chopped basil (dried or fresh)
1 large clove of garlic, crushed	1 teaspoon oregano
1/2 large green pepper, finely chopped	1 tablespoon sherry
1/2 lb (225g) lean minced beef	salt and pepper
1 1-lb, 12-oz (793g) tin Italian tomatoes	4 oz (100g) sweet *chorizo* sausage (failing that, ordinary sausage, cooked and sliced)
2 tablespoons tomato purée	

Heat the oil in a large, heavy saucepan and cook the onion and garlic slowly until the onion is golden. Add the green pepper and, when beginning to soften, push the vegetables to one side and brown the meat quickly. Add the tomatoes and their juice, breaking them up with a wooden spoon. Add the tomato purée, sugar, herbs, sherry, sausage and a good seasoning of salt and pepper. Simmer gently, uncovered, for 30–45 minutes or until the sauce is thick, stirring occasionally. Taste and correct the seasoning. (Cool and reheat later, if you prefer.)

Cook the spaghetti in a large pot of boiling, salted water until *al dente*. Drain well and season generously. Tip into a hot serving dish, pour the sauce into the middle and serve with grated Parmesan.

Serves 8

◑ 15 minutes   ◉ 50 minutes   ◔ sauce only   ▲▲

Baked Macaroni with Asparagus and Ham

1 1/2 oz (40g) butter	a little grated nutmeg
1 oz (25g) flour	salt and pepper
1 12-oz (350g) tin asparagus pieces	1 tablespoon chopped fresh parsley or chervil *or* 1/2 tablespoon dried
juice from the asparagus made up to 1 1/4 pints (725ml) with milk	1/2 lb (225g) honey roast ham, shredded
3 oz (75g) grated farmhouse Cheddar	1/2 lb (225g) macaroni
4 tablespoons grated Parmesan	5–6 tablespoons dried wholemeal breadcrumbs
	1 oz (25g) butter to finish

Melt the butter in a medium saucepan and stir in the flour. Cook for a minute or two, then take off the heat and gradually blend in the asparagus juice and milk. Stir over a moderate heat until it boils. Simmer gently for several minutes (it will thicken slightly but not much). Add the Cheddar and Parmesan and stir until well blended (making sure that it doesn't boil). Season with grated nutmeg, salt and pepper. Fold in the chopped parsley, asparagus pieces and ham, then keep over a very low heat.

Cook the macaroni in plenty of salted boiling water, until *al dente*, then drain well. Shake off any excess water, then season with salt and pepper. Blend into the sauce, then taste and correct the seasoning. Put into a shallow, lightly buttered baking dish. Scatter the breadcrumbs evenly over the top and dot with butter.* Bake in a preheated oven (375°F/Gas Mark 5/190°C) for 30–40 minutes or until nicely browned and bubbling.

Serves 6

◑ 10 minutes   ◉ 20 minutes + 35 minutes (oven)   ◔ to *   ▲▲

Lasagne

$^{1}/_{2}$ lb (225g) flat pasta for lasagne (preferably green)
$2^{1}/_{2}$ oz (65g) grated Parmesan *or* Cheddar and Parmesan mixed

1 oz (25g) butter and chopped herbs to finish

Meat Sauce
1 oz (25g) butter
2 tablespoons olive oil
6 oz (175g) finely chopped onion
1 large carrot, finely chopped
1 large stalk celery, finely chopped
1 lb (450g) lean minced beef
$^{1}/_{4}$ pint (150ml) red wine (failing that, beef stock)

$^{1}/_{4}$ pint (150ml) milk
1 14-oz (400g) tin Italian tomatoes
1 teaspoon each of basil and oregano or marjoram
pinch of sugar
salt and pepper

Béchamel Sauce
$2^{1}/_{2}$ oz (65g) butter
$2^{1}/_{2}$ oz (65g) flour
$1^{3}/_{4}$ pints (1 litre) milk

few sprigs of parsley, large slice of onion
salt, pepper, grated nutmeg

Make the meat sauce by cooking the onion in the butter and oil until soft and transparent. Add the carrot and celery and cook for 10 minutes longer. Push them to one side and brown the meat quickly. Add the wine and boil rapidly until it has disappeared. Stir in the milk and cook until it has evaporated. Add the tomatoes and their juice, breaking them up with a wooden spoon. Add the herbs, sugar, salt and pepper. Stir well, then simmer for at least 45 minutes. Taste and correct the seasoning.

Melt the butter for the béchamel in a heavy pan and stir in the flour. Cook for a minute, then remove from the heat and gradually blend in $1^{1}/_{2}$ pints (850ml) of milk. Add the parsley and onion, then season well with salt, pepper and nutmeg. Stir over gentle heat until the sauce thickens and boils. Simmer gently for several minutes then scoop out the parsley and onion.

Cook the pasta in plenty of boiling, salted water until *al dente*. Drain well, then spread out on kitchen paper to dry. Generously butter a large square baking dish or 2 smaller ones. Spread 1–2 tablespoons of the béchamel in the bottom of the dish. Cover with strips of pasta, cut to fit the dish (don't put them up the sides – they'll only get dry and brown). Put a few dollops of meat, a little béchamel and scattering of cheese on top. Repeat the layers until you get to the top, then whisk the last $^{1}/_{4}$ pint (150ml) of milk into what remains of the béchamel and pour over. Finish with the remaining cheese, light dusting of herbs and knobs of butter. Cover until needed, then bake in a hot oven (425°F/Gas Mark 7/220°C) for 20–30 minutes (removing the foil for the last 10 minutes) until hot and bubbly round the edges.

Serves 8

 20 minutes   55 minutes + 25 minutes (oven)   ◑ ▲▲

77

Cannelloni

8 oz (225g) cannelloni tubes (ready-to-bake)

chopped parsley or chervil

Spinach Filling

1 oz (25g) butter
6 oz (175g) finely chopped onion
1 large clove of garlic, crushed
1 lb (450g) cooked spinach, finely chopped

1/2 lb (225g) ricotta cheese or sieved cottage cheese
4 tablespoons Parmesan cheese
salt and pepper
freshly grated nutmeg

Sauce

2 oz (50g) butter
2 oz (50g) flour
1 teaspoon pale French mustard
2 pints (1.1 litres) milk

4 oz (100g) good Cheddar, grated
3 tablespoons grated Parmesan
salt, pepper, nutmeg

Melt the butter for the filling in a heavy pan and cook the onion and garlic until transparent. Mix in the well-drained spinach, ricotta and Parmesan. Stir until the cheese has melted, then season well with salt, pepper and nutmeg.

Melt the butter for the sauce in a saucepan and stir in the flour and mustard. Cook for a minute or two, then, off the heat, slowly blend in half the milk. Gradually bring up to the boil, stirring all the time. Simmer gently, then blend in the remaining milk. Add the cheese, and stir until it has melted completely. Season with salt, pepper and nutmeg.

Butter a large, square baking dish. Fill the cannelloni tubes with the spinach mixture and arrange in a single layer. Coat with the cheese sauce and lightly dust with parsley. Cover with foil and bake in a preheated oven (350°F/Gas Mark 4/180°C) for 1 1/2 hours (removing the foil for the last 30 minutes) or until very hot and bubbling.

Serves 6

🥄 25 minutes ⬛ 30 minutes + 1 1/2 hours (oven) ◀ ▲▲

Pilau Rice

If you want to make this rather special, add a tablespoon of chopped pistachio nuts just before serving.

2 oz (50g) butter
6 oz (175g) finely chopped onion
6 oz (175g) long-grain rice
1/2 level teaspoon ground turmeric

1/2 teaspoon ground coriander
1/2 teaspoon ground cinnamon
6 whole cloves
3/4 pint (425ml) chicken stock
1/2 teaspoon salt

Melt the butter in a large, heavy saucepan and sauté the onion until golden. Add the rice and the spices and stir until the rice becomes translucent. Pour in the stock, bring up to the boil, add the salt and stir once. Cover with a tight-fitting lid and simmer gently for 20–25 minutes or until all the stock has been absorbed. Remove from the heat and leave with the lid on for 5–10 minutes. Then remove the cloves and fork into a hot serving dish.

Serves 4

🥄5 minutes ⬛30 minutes   Steaming time: 10 minutes ◀

Saffron Rice with Nuts and Raisins

¹/2 oz (15g) butter
2 oz (50g) finely chopped
  onion
6 oz (175g) long-grain rice
pinch of saffron (failing that,
  use a little turmeric)

³/4 pint (425ml) chicken stock
  or water
salt
3 oz (75g) dry roasted peanuts
3 oz (75g) sultanas or raisins
pepper

Melt the butter in a large, heavy saucepan and sauté the onion until soft and transparent. Stir in the rice and cook until translucent. Dissolve a good pinch of saffron in a little of the stock and pour into the pan with the rest of the stock. Bring up to the boil, stir once, then cover and reduce the heat. Simmer gently for 20 minutes or until all the stock has been absorbed.* Quickly fork in the peanuts and raisins, then leave covered for 10 minutes off the heat.

Season to taste with black pepper and more salt if needed, then tip into a hot dish and serve.

Serves 4–6

◗ 5 minutes   ◉ 25 minutes   Steaming time: 10 minutes
◑ to *

Vegetable Fried Rice

This is not a trifling side-dish but a filling, delightful meal in its own right.

1 oz (25g) butter
2–4 tablespoons vegetable oil
2 rashers back bacon, finely
  diced
10 spring onions, topped,
  tailed and halved
¹/2 lb (225g) carrots, peeled
  and cut into thin strips
¹/2 lb (225g) courgettes, cut
  into thin strips
¹/2 lb (225g) mushrooms,
  sliced thickly

6 large leaves of Cos lettuce,
  rinsed, drained and
  shredded
1¹/2 tablespoons soy sauce
¹/2 tablespoon lemon juice
1 teaspoon sugar
1 lb (450g) cooked rice (6¹/2
  oz/190g uncooked weight)
salt and pepper

Melt the butter and 2 tablespoons of oil in a large, heavy sauté or frying pan. Add the bacon dice and cook for about 5 minutes or until almost crisp. Then add the onions, carrots and courgettes and stir-fry over high heat until they are *al dente* (this will take about 5 minutes), adding more oil if needed. Add the mushrooms and lettuce and cook for a further 5 minutes. Mix the soy sauce, lemon juice and sugar together in a small cup. Pour over the vegetables, then add the rice with a good seasoning of salt and pepper. Stir carefully until the rice is well coated in the sauce and piping hot. Serve at once or leave until needed, then reheat very quickly.

Serves 4

 15 minutes   20 minutes   ✱

Risotto Milanese

A rich, creamy mixture which needs patient stirring.

2 oz (50g) butter
1 small onion, peeled and
  finely chopped (about
  4 oz/100g weight)
1/2 teaspoon meat glaze or
  Bovril
12 oz (350g) round-grain
  Italian risotto rice (*arborio*)
1/4 pint (150ml) dry white
  wine

2 pints (1.1 litres) chicken
  stock
good pinch of saffron (failing
  that, use pinch of turmeric)
1 oz (25g) grated Parmesan
  cheese
chopped parsley or chervil

Melt half the butter in a large, heavy pan and add the onion. Cook until golden, then add the meat glaze and the rice. Stir until the grains are well coated with butter. Pour in the wine and boil rapidly until it has almost disappeared. Put the chicken stock into a saucepan over moderate heat. Pour 1/4 pint (150ml) of it into the rice and stir once or twice. Keep the pan over a moderate heat and, when the stock has been absorbed, add another 1/4 pint and so on until only 1/4 pint (150ml) remains. Then dissolve the saffron in a few tablespoons of the stock and pour into the pan. Stir with a wooden fork, then pour in the remaining stock. Continue stirring until the rice is tender and very creamy. Blend in the remaining butter and the grated Parmesan. Season to taste with salt and pepper, then give a light dusting of chopped parsley or chervil. Serve immediately with cold lamb, beef or ham, or just a fresh tomato salad.

Serves 4

🌢 5 minutes   ◉ 35 minutes

Creole Rice with Prawns

6 1/2 oz (190g) long-grain rice
1 oz (25g) butter
4 rashers back bacon, finely
  diced
4 oz (100g) finely chopped
  onion
12 fl oz (350ml) chicken stock
1 14-oz (400g) tin Italian
  tomatoes, drained of juice

1 teaspoon Worcestershire
  sauce
1/4 teaspoon cayenne pepper
1/2 teaspoon ground mace
2 tablespoons finely chopped
  parsley
1/2 lb (225g) peeled, cooked
  prawns
salt and pepper

Wash the rice under cold running water and leave to drain in a sieve.

Melt *half* the butter in a large, flameproof casserole and cook the bacon dice until very crisp. Add the remaining butter and the onion and cook until the onion is almost golden (stirring frequently). Add the rice and stir until it becomes translucent. Pour in the stock and the tomatoes, breaking them up with the side of a wooden spoon. Add the Worcestershire sauce, cayenne pepper, ground mace and half the parsley. Bring up to the boil, then cover and transfer to a moderate oven (350°F/Gas Mark 4/180°C). Bake for 30 minutes, then take out and fork in the prawns. Cover and return to the oven. Cook for 10–15 minutes longer or until the liquid has been absorbed. Take out of the oven and leave for 10–15 minutes without removing the lid. Season to taste with salt and freshly ground black pepper, then scatter the remaining parsley over the top.

Serves 2–3, or 4 if served with a salad

🌢 5 minutes   ◉ 15 minutes + 45 minutes (oven)
Steaming time: 10 minutes

Pies, Pancakes, Pizzas

Tomatoes, cheese and herbs bring out the best in each other and, when found in the same oven, produce an aroma that is patently seductive. It draws guests to the kitchen more effectively than any dinner gong.

Restaurants like the Pizza Express have dramatically raised pizza expectations in this country and the Chicago Pizza Pie Factory in London has staked its reputation on a deep-dish variety with filling an inch thick. The limp imitation – with its paltry scraps of salami and cheese – seems, mercifully, on the wane. It would hardly have stretched round a supper table but the real *pizza* – oozing with tomatoes and cheese – is a hearty meal in itself.

To make it at home, commandeer half the bread dough or make one specially (page 89). If the screaming hordes are about to descend, make a quick scone dough instead or use crisp French bread. Having done this, the pizza will only be as good as the bits you put on it. Start with a tomato base, then add any of the following: sautéed onions, mushrooms, green pepper, pepperoni, sausage, shredded ham, olives, anchovies, capers, artichoke hearts, cheese (Mozzarella, Parmesan or Cheddar).

The crisp pizza crust is produced by cooking it on the fired-earth floor of a bread oven. This can be partly simulated at home by putting a large terracotta tile on your oven shelf. When the oven is really hot (450°C/Gas Mark 8/230°C), slide the pizza in its tin or tray on to the tile.

Quiches and pies make superb supper dishes and, unlike the temperamental soufflé, won't deflate if kept waiting. A quiche can be endlessly varied, using different bases (wholemeal, wheatmeal, plain shortcrust or puff) and middles. Pre-baking the shell in a hot oven (425°F/Gas Mark 7/220°C) ensures that it remains crisp – even under the soggiest mixture. Toasted, chopped walnuts or hazelnuts add further crunch and taste to shortcrust pastry and are particularly good if the filling contains spinach or ham.

Individual pies or pasties are tailor-made for the family that turns up at different times for supper. They freeze well and can easily be reheated. They're good candidates for suppers eaten *en route* – especially pasties, as they're fairly indestructible and keep warm for a long time.

Pancakes are too good to be reserved for Shrove Tuesday and desserts only. When made with wholewheat flour (the closest thing to the Breton *crêpe au sarrasin*) they provide a delicious vehicle for ratatouille, cheese and ham, bacon and courgettes or creamed smoked haddock.

Watercress and Walnut Quiche

6 oz (175g) shortcrust pastry
1¹/₂ oz (40g) butter
8 good-sized spring onions,
   topped, tailed and chopped
2 bunches of watercress,
   shredded
3 oz (75g) cream cheese

2 large eggs
2 oz (50g) Cheddar, grated
5 fl oz (150ml) single cream
salt, pepper and nutmeg
2 oz (50g) toasted walnuts,
   finely chopped

Roll out the pastry and use to line an 8-inch (20cm) flan ring or tin. Prick the base lightly with a fork. Line with a circle of greaseproof paper and fill with baking beans. Bake in a preheated oven (425°F/Gas Mark 7/220°C) for 12 minutes, then remove the paper and beans and bake for a further 5–7 minutes.

Melt half the butter in a heavy pan and sauté the onions until soft. Add the watercress with the remaining butter and cook for several minutes. Put the onion, watercress and pan juices into a liquidizer or food processor and blend for several seconds.

Put the cream cheese into a bowl and work with a fork until soft. Beat the eggs lightly and gradually blend into the cheese with the cream. Season well with salt, black pepper and freshly grated nutmeg. (Alternatively, this could all be done in one step in a food processor.) Blend in half the watercress purée, the grated cheese and half the walnuts. Taste and correct the seasoning if necessary.

Transfer the mixture to the flan case and top with the remaining purée, cheese and walnuts. Bake at 375°F/Gas Mark 5/190°C for about 25 minutes or until set and lightly browned. Serve warm or cold.

Serves 6

◖ 20 minutes ◙ 45 minutes (oven) + 10 minutes ◗ ▲▲

Quiche Paysanne

Wholemeal pastry gives this quiche an extra fillip.

6 oz (175g) wholemeal or
   plain shortcrust pastry
2 oz (50g) butter
1 medium onion, peeled and
   finely sliced
4 rashers back bacon, finely
   diced
4 oz (100g) button
   mushrooms, finely diced

¹/₂ lb (225g) cooked potato,
   thinly sliced
salt and pepper
2 large eggs
¹/₄ pint (150ml) single cream
2 oz (50g) mature Cheddar,
   grated
a little chopped parsley

Roll out the pastry and use to line an 8-inch (20cm) flan ring or tin. Prick the base lightly with a fork, then line with a circle of greaseproof paper and fill with baking beans. Bake in a preheated oven (425°F/Gas Mark 7/220°C) for 12 minutes, then remove the paper and beans and bake for a further 5–7 minutes. Take out and put to one side.

Melt half the butter in a large frying pan. Add the onion and bacon and cook until the onion is golden, the bacon crisp. Add the mushrooms and cook until they have darkened in colour. Push the vegetables to one side, then add the remaining butter with the potato slices. Cook for a further 10 minutes until the potatoes are lightly browned. Season well with salt and pepper.

Beat the eggs lightly, blend in the cream and season well. Spread the vegetable mixture over the base of the flan case. Pour over the beaten eggs and top with the grated cheese and parsley. Bake at 375°F/Gas Mark 5/190°C for about 25 minutes or until set. Take out and serve warm with a crisp green salad.

Serves 6

◖ 20 minutes ◙ 45 minutes (oven) + 20 minutes ◗ ▲▲

Spring Onion Quiche

If spring onions are nowhere to be found, use 2 medium onions cooked in plenty of butter until golden.

6 oz (175g) shortcrust pastry (plain or wholemeal)
1½ bunches of spring onions (about 15), topped and tailed
1½ oz (40g) butter

3 large eggs
5 fl oz (150ml) single cream
3 oz (75g) good Cheddar, grated
salt and pepper

Roll out the pastry and use to line an 8-inch (20cm) flan ring or tin. Prick the base lightly, then line with greaseproof paper and fill with baking beans. Bake in a preheated oven (425°F/Gas Mark 7/220°C) for 12 minutes, then remove the paper and beans and bake for 5–7 minutes longer. Take out and put to one side.

As the pastry bakes, begin the filling. Roughly chop the spring onions, including the green ends. Melt the butter in a heavy pan and cook the onions slowly until soft and almost golden. Beat the eggs lightly, blend in the cream, onions and half the Cheddar. Season to taste with salt and pepper.

Pour the filling carefully into the flan case. Top with the remaining cheese and bake at 375°F/Gas Mark 5/190°C for 25–30 minutes or until set. Take out and serve warm with watercress and brown bread.

Serves 6

🥄 20 minutes ◼ 45 minutes (oven) + 10 minutes ◗ ▲▲

Spinach and Cottage Cheese Quiche

The dramatic red and green of this quiche make it ideal for the Christmas season or for any meal that needs a perk.

6 oz (175g) shortcrust pastry
1 oz (25g) butter
3 oz (75g) finely chopped onion
½ lb (225g) frozen chopped spinach, thawed completely
salt and black pepper
freshly grated nutmeg

3 medium eggs
½ lb (225g) cottage cheese
4 tablespoons milk
3 tablespoons freshly grated Parmesan
2 small ripe tomatoes
½ oz (15g) butter

Roll out the pastry and use to line an 8-inch (20cm) flan ring or tin. Prick the base lightly, line with greaseproof paper and fill with baking beans. Bake in a preheated oven (425°F/Gas Mark 7/220°C) for 12 minutes, then remove the paper and beans and bake for a further 5–7 minutes.

Melt the butter in a heavy pan and sauté the onion until golden. Drain the spinach well, then mix in. Cook for about 5 minutes or until quite dry. Season well with salt, pepper and nutmeg.

Liquidize the eggs, cottage cheese, milk and Parmesan cheese until smooth, then season to taste. Scrape out into the spinach pan and fold in until thoroughly blended. Transfer to the pastry case, spreading out evenly with a spatula. Slice the tomatoes into thin, crosswise slices, then cut in half. Arrange these as a border around the outside edge, with the rounded sides pointing towards the centre. Dot the top of the filling with knobs of butter and put into a moderately hot oven (375°F/Gas Mark 5/190°C) for 25–30 minutes or until set. Serve warm with a tomato salad.

Serves 6

🥄 20 minutes ◼ 50 minutes (oven) + 15 minutes ◗ ▲▲

Pissaladière

6 oz (175g) rich shortcrust
   pastry
1 2-oz (50g) tin anchovy
   fillets, well drained of oil
2 tablespoons milk
1 oz (25g) butter
1 tablespoon olive or vegetable
   oil
1 large onion, peeled and
   thinly sliced

1 14-oz (400g) tin Italian
   tomatoes
pinch of sugar
$1/2$ teaspoon each of dried
   marjoram, basil and
   oregano
salt and pepper
6 black olives
chopped fresh basil or
   marjoram (optional)

Roll out the pastry to a large rectangle. Lightly grease a baking tray and put the pastry on it. Prick all over with a fork, then bake in a preheated oven (425°F/Gas Mark 7/220°C) for 15–20 minutes, until pale golden.

Put the anchovy fillets in a saucer and cover with milk. Leave for 15 minutes, then drain well.

As the pastry bakes, begin the filling. Heat the butter and oil in a heavy pan and sauté the onion until golden. Add the tomatoes and their juice, breaking them up with a wooden spoon. Add a pinch of sugar, the herbs, salt and pepper. Continue cooking for 10–15 minutes until the mixture is a thick (but not dry) purée. Taste and correct the seasoning.

Spread the tomato mixture over the pastry base, leaving a $1/4$-inch (.50cm) border all the way round. Top with a lattice of anchovy fillets. Halve the black olives and fill the 'diamonds' made by the anchovies with these (one half per 'diamond'). Scatter the basil (if used) over the top and bake at 375°F/Gas Mark 5/190°C for 20 minutes, then move nearer the top of the oven for 10–15 minutes longer. Slice and eat warm with a green salad.

Serves 6

◗ 15 minutes ▣ 50 minutes (oven) + 20 minutes ◐ ▲▲

84

Leek and Ham Pie

A speciality of Picardie, this golden puff of leeks and cream makes others pies pale by comparison.

3 oz (75g) butter
4 oz (100g) peeled and thinly
   sliced onion
1 lb (450g) leeks, halved
   lengthwise and chopped
2 oz (50g) ham, finely
   shredded

2 egg yolks
4 fl oz (100ml) double cream
salt and black pepper
13 oz (375g) puff pastry
lightly beaten egg

Melt half the butter in a heavy pan and cook the onion slowly until golden. Blend in the remaining butter and the leeks, then partly cover the pan and cook quickly until the leeks have softened and almost all the liquid has evaporated. Add the ham, then blend in the yolks and cream (mixed together first). Season well with salt and pepper, then cool.

Divide the pastry in half and roll out two circles, one slightly bigger than the other. Use the larger of the two to line a lightly buttered 8-inch (20cm) flan ring, placed on a greased baking tray. Fill with the cooled leek mixture and top with the remaining pastry. Pinch the edges together, flute and cut a small hole in the centre. Decorate the top by marking thin lines spiralling out from the centre to the outside edge. Chill well, then brush the top with lightly beaten egg and bake at 425°F/Gas Mark 7/220°C for 10–15 minutes, then at 375°F/Gas Mark 5/190°C for 20–25 minutes or until nicely puffed and golden. Take out and leave for 5 minutes, then carefully remove the flan ring and cut into wedges.

Serves 6

◗ 20 minutes ▣ 30 minutes (oven) + 20 minutes ◐ ▲▲

Chicken Cobbler

4 large cooked chicken breasts
    or 1 3-lb (1.5 kilos) cooked
    chicken
2¹/₂ oz (65g) butter
1 medium onion, peeled and
    chopped
2 oz (50g) flour

1 pint (575ml) chicken stock
¹/₂ pint (275ml) milk
1 tablespoon chopped parsley
6 oz (175g) carrots, cooked
    and cut into thin strips
6 oz (175g) peas, cooked
salt and pepper

Cobbler Topping
¹/₂ lb (225g) plain flour
2 level teaspoons baking
    powder

¹/₂ level teaspoon salt
2 oz (50g) butter
¹/₄ pint (150ml) milk

Skin and bone the chicken and cut into bite-size chunks.

Melt ¹/₂ oz (15g) butter in a heavy pan, cook the onion until soft, then lift out with a slotted spoon. Add the remaining butter, stir in the flour and cook for a minute. Remove from the heat and gradually blend in the stock and milk. Stir over moderate heat until it boils. Simmer for several minutes, then add the parsley, carrots, peas and chicken chunks. Season with salt and pepper, then put in a large gratin or baking dish.*

Sift the flour, baking powder and salt into a large bowl and rub in the butter. Make a well in the centre, pour in the milk and mix to a soft dough. Knead gently, then roll out to fit the dish (the dough should rest inside the dish, rather than on the rim). Brush lightly with milk, then score in a lattice pattern. Bake in a hot oven (400°F/Gas Mark 6/200°C) for 30–40 minutes or until golden brown.

Serves 6

🥄 20 minutes ◼ 15 minutes + 30 minutes (oven) ◐ to *

SC - FR

Humble Pie

Humble only because it uses leftovers.

4 oz (100g) finely chopped
    onion
1 oz (25g) butter
1¹/₂ large stalks celery, finely
    chopped
1 crisp apple, peeled and
    finely chopped
large pinch of sugar
1 lb (450g) leftover cooked
    pork, minced

¹/₄ pint (150ml) beef stock or
    equivalent amount of gravy
    and water mixed
generous pinches of mixed
    spice and ground cinnamon
salt and black pepper
8 oz (225g) shortcrust or puff
    pastry
beaten egg to glaze

Sauté the onion in the butter until soft. Add the celery, apple and sugar and cook for 10 minutes, stirring occasionally. Add the meat and stock and simmer uncovered for 10–15 minutes, to evaporate most of the stock. Add the spices and season well.

Let the mixture cool slightly, then transfer to a lightly greased, deep, 9-inch (22.5cm) pie dish, spreading it out evenly. Put a blackbird in the middle if you have one. Roll out the pastry until it is ¹/₂ inch (.50cm) larger all the way round than the diameter of the dish. Cut a ¹/₂-inch (.50cm) strip from the outside edge. Dampen the edge of the dish with water and place the strip on it. Dampen this and lower the rest of the pastry on top. Trim the edges, then pinch to seal and crimp decoratively. Cut a hole in the centre (if a blackbird isn't used) and chill. Brush the top with lightly beaten egg, then bake in a preheated oven at 425°F/Gas Mark 7/220°C for 20 minutes, then at 375°F/Gas Mark 5/190°C for a further 20–30 minutes.

Serves 4

🥄 20 minutes ◼ 30 minutes + 45 minutes (oven) ◐ ▲▲

Fisherman's Pie

³/₄ lb (350g) fresh haddock or
  cod fillets
3 oz (75g) butter
salt and pepper
¹/₂ medium onion, peeled and
  finely chopped
2 large carrots, peeled and cut
  into strips
2 large leeks, washed and
  chopped

¹/₂ pint (275ml) chicken stock
¹/₂ lb (225g) button
  mushrooms, thickly sliced
1 oz (25g) flour
about ¹/₂ pint (275ml) milk
4 oz (100g) cooked, peeled
  prawns
1 rounded tablespoon chopped
  parsley
lightly beaten egg

Dot the haddock with 1 oz (25g) of the butter and season well. Bake in a moderate oven for 15–20 minutes then lift out carefully (leaving the skin behind) and put into a large, deep pie dish. Sieve the pan juices into a measuring jug.

Cook the onion in another ounce (25g) of butter until almost golden. Add the carrots, leeks and about 4 fl oz (100ml) of the stock. Simmer partly covered for 10 minutes, then add the mushrooms and simmer for a few minutes longer. Lift all the vegetables out with a slotted spoon and tip the juices into the rest of the chicken stock. Add the remaining butter to the pan and stir in the flour. Cook for a minute, then gradually blend in the stock and the fish juices made up to ¹/₂ pint (275ml) with milk. Stir until it thickens and boils, then add the prawns, vegetables and parsley. Season and fold carefully into the fish in the pie dish. Roll out the pastry to fit the dish, place on top and pinch the edges to seal. Cut a hole in the centre and brush the top with beaten egg. Bake at 425°F/Gas Mark 7/220°F for 20 minutes, then at 375°F/Gas Mark 5/190°C for a further 20–25 minutes.

Serves 6

◕ 15 minutes ◉ 1 hour (oven) + 25 minutes ◀
▲▲ (unbaked)

86

Beef 'Jalousie'

1 oz (25g) butter
¹/₂ large onion, peeled and
  finely chopped
5 oz (150g) carrots, peeled and
  diced
1 fat clove of garlic, crushed
³/₄ lb (350g) lean minced beef

¹/₂ pint (275ml) beef stock
2 large ripe tomatoes, roughly
  chopped
1 tablespoon chopped parsley
salt and pepper
14 oz (400g) puff pastry
beaten egg to glaze

Sauté the onion, carrots and garlic in the butter until the onion is golden. Push to one side, then brown the beef quickly. Blend in the stock, the tomatoes and their juice, the parsley and a good seasoning of salt and pepper. Cook uncovered for 20 minutes or until thick but not dry. Cool.

Cut the pastry in half and roll out thinly until you have two long rectangles about 12 inches (30cm) long and 7 inches (17.5cm) wide (one just slightly larger than the other). Take the larger one and fold in half lengthwise. Cut horizontal slits in it – about ¹/₂ inch (1cm) apart and slightly less than ¹/₂ inch (1cm) from the outside edge. Place the uncut rectangle on a buttered baking tray. Spread the meat filling over it, leaving a border of just under ¹/₂ inch (1cm) all the way round. Moisten the edges with beaten egg and place the cut rectangle on top. Fold the edges under the bottom rectangle, then, with the back of a knife, press a deep line just under ¹/₂ inch (1cm) from the outside edge all the way round. Then mark this border at ¹/₄-inch (.50cm) intervals with the back of a knife to seal the pastry. Chill, then brush with beaten egg and bake in a preheated oven (425°F/Gas Mark 7/220°C) for 20 minutes, then for a further 10–20 minutes at 375°F/Gas Mark 5/190°C.

Serves 4

◕ 20 minutes ◉ 25 minutes + 30 minutes (oven)
▲▲ (unbaked)

Beefsteak, Kidney and Mushroom Pie

1 lb (450g) stewing beef	2 level tablespoons flour
1/2 lb (225g) kidneys	3/4 pint (425ml) beef stock
3 oz (75g) butter	1/2 pint (275ml) red wine
1 tablespoon vegetable oil	3 tablespoons port (optional)
1 medium onion, peeled and	salt and pepper
chopped	8 oz (225g) puff pastry
1/2 lb (225g) mushrooms	beaten egg

Trim the meat and cut into medium chunks. Trim the kidneys and halve. Heat 1 oz (25g) of the butter with the oil in a large, heavy saucepan. Quickly brown the beef and kidneys, then lift out with a slotted spoon.

Add another 1 oz (25g) of butter and cook the onion until soft. Add the remaining butter with the mushrooms and cook until they have softened. Sprinkle the flour on top and cook for a minute. Gradually stir in the stock, red wine and port (if used). Return the meat to the pan and season with salt and pepper. Cover and simmer gently, stirring occasionally, for 1 1/4–1 1/2 hours or until the meat is tender. Correct the seasoning, then put into a deep pie dish.

Roll out the pastry 1/2 inch (1cm) larger all the way round than the dish. Cut off a 1/2-inch (1cm) strip from the outside edge and place on the rim of the dish (moistened first with water). Dampen this, then place the pastry on top, crimping the edges to seal. Cut a hole in the centre and prick the top lightly. Chill, then brush with beaten egg and bake at 425°F/Gas Mark 7/220°C for 15–20 minutes, then at 375°F/Gas Mark 5/190°F for a further 15–20 minutes or until well risen and golden.

Serves 6

➥ 15 minutes   ▣ 1 1/4 hours + 35 minutes (oven)   ◕
▲▲ (unbaked)

Crispy Pancakes with Ratatouille Filling

10–12 small pancakes,	1 1/2 oz (40g) melted butter
preferably wholewheat	4–6 tablespoons grated
(page 121)	Cheddar or Gruyère

Filling

1 medium aubergine	4 large ripe tomatoes,
salt	quartered
8 oz (225g) peeled and	good pinch of sugar
chopped onion	1 teaspoon chopped basil
1 1/2 oz (40g) butter	(fresh or dried)
2 tablespoons olive or	pepper
vegetable oil	few tablespoons of red wine or
1 lb (450g) courgettes, sliced	stock

Halve the aubergine, score the flesh with a knife and salt generously. Place between two plates and weight the top. Leave for at least 30 minutes, then rinse and pat dry with kitchen paper. Cut into medium chunks.

Cook the onion in 1 1/2 oz (40g) butter until golden, then push to one side and add the oil, with the aubergine chunks. Cook quickly until lightly browned. Add the courgettes, tomatoes with their juice, sugar, basil, salt and pepper and wine. Cook, stirring occasionally, until the mixture is quite thick, but not dry (about 20–25 minutes). Season to taste.

Put a thick strip of the filling down the middle of each pancake and fold up like a parcel (making a long rectangle). Place close together in a buttered, shallow baking tin or gratin dish. Brush with melted butter and scatter the cheese over the top. Put into a hot oven (400°F/Gas Mark 6/200°C) until crisp and lightly browned (about 20–30 minutes).

Serves 5–6

➥ 30 minutes   ▣ 30 minutes + 30 minutes (oven)   ◕ ▲▲

Wholemeal Vegetable Pasties

³/₄ lb (350g) wholemeal pastry

Filling

1¹/₂ oz (40g) butter
1 medium onion, peeled and thinly sliced
3 large carrots, scrubbed and cut into medium chunks
³/₄ lb (350g) peeled and chopped swede
4 large leeks, cleaned and cut into chunks
¹/₄ pint (150ml) chicken stock
salt and pepper
4 oz (100g) good Cheddar, grated
beaten egg or milk

Make the pastry, then quarter. Roll each one out thinly into a circle roughly 7 inches (17.5cm) in diameter. Layer up with large pieces of greaseproof paper and chill.

Sauté the onion in the butter until golden. Add the carrots, swede and leeks and toss well in the buttery juices. Pour in the stock, then cover with a buttered paper and lid. Cook for 15 minutes or until the carrots and swede are just tender. Season well with salt and pepper, stir once or twice, then cool.

Dampen the edges of the pastry circles with water or beaten egg. Put a few generous spoonfuls of the vegetable mixture down the middle of each one and top with a light grating of cheese (you'll probably need all the vegetable mixture as the pasties should be very plump). Bring the edges together and crimp to seal.   Make a few slashes in the top and brush all over with milk or lightly beaten egg. Bake in a preheated oven (425°F/Gas Mark 7/220°C) for 15 minutes, then at 375°F/Gas Mark 5/190°C for a further 30–40 minutes. Serve warm with a green salad.

Serves 4

◗ 20 minutes   ▣ 20 minutes + 45 minutes (oven)   ◑ ▲

Crespolini

Ordinary pancakes suddenly become a rather dashing supper dish.

10 crisp pancakes (page 121)
2–3 oz (50–75g) melted butter
4 oz (100g) grated cheese (half Parmesan, half Cheddar)

Filling

1 lb (450g) chopped cooked spinach, well drained
6 oz (175g) cream cheese
1 tablespoon grated Parmesan
3 large slices cooked ham, finely shredded
salt and pepper
freshly grated nutmeg

Mix the spinach, cream cheese and Parmesan in a large bowl until smooth and thoroughly blended (or do this in a food processor or liquidizer). Fold in the shredded ham and season well with salt, pepper and a little grated nutmeg. Put a generous spoonful of this mixture in the centre of each pancake and roll up. Place side by side in a well buttered gratin dish.

When ready to cook the dish, pour over the melted butter and scatter the cheese evenly on top. Put into a hot oven (400°F/Gas Mark 6/200°C) for 15–20 minutes or until hot, bubbling and golden brown. (Alternatively, you could coat the pancakes in a thin béchamel sauce and top with half the above quantity of cheese. Delicious, but very rich.) Take out and serve with a green salad.

Serves 4

◗ 20 minutes   ▣ 20 minutes

Chicago-style Pizza

¹/₄ oz (7g) fresh yeast *or* 1 level teaspoon dried yeast plus ¹/₂ level teaspoon sugar
¹/₂ pint lukewarm water

1 lb (450g) plain flour
³/₄ teaspoon salt
good pinch of sugar
2 tablespoons olive oil

Filling
2 14-oz (400g) tins Italian tomatoes
4 tablespoons tomato purée
pinch of castor sugar
¹/₂ teaspoon each of dried marjoram, basil and oregano

salt and pepper
6–8 oz (175–225g) sausage or salami, chopped
12 oz (350g) Mozzarella cheese

Dissolve the yeast in the warm water. Sift the flour, salt and sugar into a large mixing bowl and blend to a soft dough with the yeast mixture and olive oil. Knead for about 5 minutes or until elastic and smooth.

Oil two round 10-inch (25cm) baking tins. Cut the dough in half and roll out to fit. Press the dough down firmly, then cover with cling-film. Leave until the dough has doubled in size, then pummel down with your knuckles, cover and allow to rise again. Pummel down, then press a thin layer up the sides of the tin.

Put the tomatoes with 4 tablespoons of their juice into a bowl with the tomato purée, sugar, herbs, salt and pepper. Break up the tomatoes and blend until you have a chunky mixture, then spread evenly over the dough. Thinly slice the Mozzarella and place on top with the sausage. Dust with more herbs if you like and brush the rim of the dough with oil. Bake in a hot oven (450°F/Gas Mark 8/230°C) for 25–30 minutes.

Makes 2 large pizzas (each serves 4–6)

 1¹/₄ hours ◙ 30 minutes ◐ ▲▲ (unbaked)

Presto Pizza

¹/₂ lb (225g) self-raising flour
¹/₂ teaspoon salt
2 oz (50g) butter

5 fl oz (150ml) milk
a little olive or vegetable oil

Filling
1 5-oz (150g) tin tomato purée
7 tablespoons water
1 teaspoon sugar
1 teaspoon dried marjoram
1 teaspoon dried oregano
1 teaspoon French mustard
3 tablespoons grated Parmesan

salt and pepper
4 oz (100g) sliced onion
1 oz (25g) butter
6 oz (175g) button mushrooms, sliced
4 oz (100g) Mozzarella or Cheddar, thinly sliced

Mix together the tomato purée, water, sugar, herbs, mustard, 1 tablespoon of Parmesan and salt and pepper to taste. Cook the onion in the butter until golden, then add the mushrooms and cook until just softened. Season with salt and pepper.

Sift the flour and salt into a large mixing bowl. Rub in the butter, then pour in the milk and mix to a soft dough. Turn out on to a lightly floured surface and knead lightly. Roll out until ¹/₈ inch (.25cm) thick and lift on to a lightly oiled baking tray or loose base (9 inches or 10 inches/22.5cm or 25cm) of a flat tin. Press down firmly, turning up the edges to prevent the sauce escaping. Brush the dough with a little oil. Spread the tomato mixture out evenly, then top with the Mozzarella or Cheddar, onions and mushrooms. Dust with the remaining Parmesan and a few chopped herbs if you like. Bake in a hot oven (450°F/Gas Mark 8/230°C), just above the centre, for about 20 minutes.

Serves 4–6

 20 minutes ◙ 10 minutes + 20 minutes (oven) ◐

Quick Snacks

This chapter is for the evenings when the cook's tired – and so is everyone else. Most of the recipes can be done in less than ten minutes – and all of them take remarkably little energy.

A freezer is invaluable to the sporadic snacker, keeping vital ingredients within easy reach – frozen pastry, bread, rolls, pizza dough, crêpes, butter, grated cheese, sausages, bacon. Any gaps can be filled by a well-stocked larder shelf which includes tomato purée, mayonnaise, chutney, Parmesan cheese, tinned salmon, tuna or sardines.

The latest snack 'sensation' to hit France and America is the filled croissant – in every conceivable combination. The long-serving *croque monsieur* is rapidly taking a back shelf to this crisp newcomer. Croissants with pâté, *aux fines herbes*, with bacon and onion, ham and cheese, cream cheese and chives – and so on, *ad indigestion*. Provided you remember to take the puff pastry out of the freezer in time, any of these could be yours within 30 minutes. Preheat the oven, roll out the pastry, cut into triangles, fill and bake. (Any left over can be popped back into the freezer until the next hunger pang strikes.)

Pancakes can be used to similarly delicious effect. Follow the instructions in the pancake chapter for thawing (or make up a fresh batch, but this requires 'resting' time), then fill. If inspiration deserts you, try the following:

apples, thick cream, cinnamon and sugar
cottage cheese, lemon juice and sugar (the Polish *blintz*)
spinach and cheese
creamed chicken
mushrooms and crisp bacon
prawns, lemon juice and cream cheese

Savoury pancakes can be sprinkled with grated cheese before they go into the oven; sweet ones, dusted with icing sugar when they come out.

A thin French *baguette* makes a good portable snack. When split and spread with a little oil, sliced tomatoes, green pepper, salami and cheese, it becomes the Niçoise sandwich – *pan bagna*. A plumper version, often sold by the foot, appears in New York as the submarine sandwich. Far better, to my mind, is a 'hot pastrami on rye' – steaming hot smoked beef stacked between dark bread, with mustard oozing out the sides.

Any crisp bread is a good foil for scrambled eggs or the cold omelette (which sounds revolting until you've tried it) that the French and Spanish are so fond of. A brioche would make a more delicate mouthful – filled with crisp bacon, tomatoes and cheese, then wrapped in foil and put into a hot oven. In summer it could be stuffed with a creamy mixture of salmon, mayonnaise and cucumber, then served cold.

Croque Monsieur

4 slices of bread from a large
  white sandwich loaf
about 1 oz (25g) soft butter
4 slices Gruyère or Cheddar
  cheese

4 slices cooked ham
2 oz (50g) butter plus 2
  tablespoons vegetable oil

Butter the bread on one side only. Cover two of them with
a slice of Gruyère and ham. Put the remaining bread slices
on top and press down firmly.

Fry the *croques* in the butter and oil until golden on both
sides.

Serves 2

◗ 5 minutes   ◉ 10 minutes

Croque Madame

4 slices of bread from a large
  white sandwich loaf
a little butter

4 slices Gruyère or Cheddar
  cheese
4 large slices tomato
4 bacon rashers, grilled

Toast the bread and butter it on one side only. Place on each
one a slice of cheese, a slice of tomato, then a bacon rasher
cut into three. Put on a baking tray and into a hot oven
(400°F/Gas Mark 6/200°C) for 15 minutes or until the
cheese is bubbling.

Serves 2

◗ 5 minutes   ◉ 15 minutes (oven)

Mozzarella in Carozza

*Mozzarella 'in a carriage', here with a little tomato to enliven the
cheese.*

4–6 oz (100–175g) Mozzarella
  cheese
8 thin slices of wholemeal
  bread
2 large ripe tomatoes, sliced

salt and pepper
fresh basil (optional)
2 eggs, lightly beaten
1 oz (25g) butter
2 tablespoons vegetable oil

Slice the Mozzarella thinly and divide between four slices of
bread. Cover with the tomato slices and season well with salt
and pepper (and a little chopped fresh basil, if you've got it).
Top with the remaining bread and press down firmly. Trim
the crusts off, then dip both sides of the sandwiches in the
lightly beaten eggs. Put on a large plate and leave for 30
minutes.

Heat the butter and 2 tablespoons of oil in a large, heavy
skillet. Fry the sandwiches on both sides until golden, adding
more oil as you need it. Take out, cut each sandwich in half
and eat at once.

Serves 4, or 2 hungrier eaters

◗ 35 minutes   ◉ 15 minutes

Toasted Bacon, Lettuce and Tomato Sandwich

Known affectionately as a 'BLT', this must be the most wonderful mixture to appear between two slices of toast.

4 slices bread cut from a large white sandwich loaf
a little butter
mayonnaise

1 large ripe tomato *or* 2 small
4 rashers back bacon
salt and black pepper
2 large leaves crisp lettuce

Toast the bread, then butter two slices on one side only. Spread the other two slices (on one side) with a little mayonnaise. Slice the tomato crosswise and grill the bacon until crisp. Put several slices of tomato on each buttered slice and top with 2 rashers of bacon. Give a generous seasoning of salt and pepper, then put the lettuce and remaining toast on top (mayonnaise side down). Press down firmly, cut each sandwich in half and eat at once.

Serves 2

🥄 10 minutes   ◉ 5 minutes

92

Club Sandwiches

Another American 'classic' which would make a quick summer supper.

4 slices of bread cut from a large white sandwich loaf
a little butter
mayonnaise
4–6 slices leftover cooked chicken

4 large tomato slices
4 rashers crisp bacon
salt and pepper
2 crisp leaves of lettuce

Toast the bread and spread two slices with butter (on one side only); the other two with mayonnaise. On top of the buttered slices, put the chicken, tomato slices and bacon. Season well with salt and pepper, then finish with the lettuce and the other two pieces of toast (mayonnaise side down). Press down firmly, cut in half and eat.

Serves 2

🥄 5 minutes   ◉ 5 minutes

French Toast

3 eggs
4 fl oz (100ml) milk
¼ teaspoon salt

2–3 oz (50–75g) butter
4–6 slices of bread

Beat the eggs, milk and salt together in a large bowl. Heat the butter in a large, heavy skillet, then dip the bread slices into the egg mixture and fry – one or two at a time – in the hot butter. When both sides are golden, lift out and serve. Those with a sweet tooth should add a teaspoon of sugar to the batter and serve the toast with maple syrup. For a savoury version, cover the ordinary French toast with crumbled crisp bacon and a little grated cheese and put under the grill until bubbling and lightly browned.

Serves 2

🍲 5 minutes   ◉ 15 minutes

Stuffed Pitta Bread

2 whole pieces *pitta* bread
  (preferably wholewheat)
2 ripe tomatoes
salt and pepper
a little butter
4 oz (100g) good Cheddar,
  grated

2 large slices cooked ham,
  shredded
a few chopped chives
  (optional)

Slice the pitta open horizontally, being careful not to cut all the way through. Roughly chop the tomatoes (into medium chunks) and season well with salt and pepper. Spread the inside of each pitta (inside bottom only) with a little butter, then fill with chopped tomatoes, grated cheese, ham and chives (if used). Fill each 'pocket' generously, then wrap the whole in foil and place on a baking tray. Put into a hot oven (400°F/Gas Mark 6/200°C) and bake for about 20 minutes (peeling the foil back for the last 5 minutes to crisp the top) or until the cheese has melted and the pitta is very hot. Take out and eat, preferably with a bib – it's very messy. But delicious.

Serves 2

🍲 10 minutes   ◉ 20 minutes (oven)

Pizza Bread

1 small French loaf about
  14 inches (35cm) long
2 oz (50g) soft butter
4 tablespoons tomato purée
6 tablespoons water
pinch of sugar
4 tablespoons Parmesan
  cheese

½ teaspoon each of dried basil
  and oregano or marjoram
salt and pepper
6 oz (175g) thinly sliced
  Cheddar or Mozzarella
4 oz (100g) cooked ham,
  bacon or sausage, shredded
  (optional)

Slice the bread in half horizontally, then cut each half in two.
Turn each piece, cut side down, on a bread board. Press
firmly with the heel of your hand to flatten, then turn right
side up and pull out any excess bread dough, leaving about
an ⅛-inch (.25cm) layer of bread covering the crust. Spread
the inside with the soft butter. Mix the tomato purée with
the water, sugar, half the Parmesan cheese and herbs.
Season with salt and pepper. Spread evenly over the bread
and top with the cheese slices and ham, bacon or sausage (if
used). Place on a lightly buttered baking tray and put into
a hot oven (400°F/Gas Mark 6/200°C) for 20–30 minutes, or
until crisp and lightly browned. Take out, allow to cool
slightly, then eat.

Serves 4

◗ 10 minutes   ◙ 25 minutes (oven)

94

Aubergine Sarnies

An unexpectedly succulent mouthful.

2 small aubergines, about 1 lb
  (450g) total weight
salt
3 large slices good Cheddar

several tablespoons olive or
  vegetable oil
pepper

Wipe the aubergines and cut in thin slices lengthwise. Salt
generously, then leave between two plates for at least 30
minutes. Rinse and pat dry with kitchen paper. Make up
sandwiches with the aubergine slices, putting a slice of
cheese between each one. Cover a grill rack with foil, then
place the 'sarnies' side by side on it. Brush the tops lightly
with oil and put under a hot grill. Grill until nicely browned,
then flip over carefully, brush with more oil and continue
grilling until golden brown. Take out, season with a little salt
and pepper, then eat.

Serves 2

◗ 35 minutes   ◙ 10 minutes

Scrambled Egg
and Hot Sausage Roll

1 small French loaf
2 oz (50g) butter
2 English sausages *or* 1 large
  continental one (*chorizo,
  saveloy* or frankfurter)

2 large eggs
splash of water
salt and pepper

Cut off two-thirds of the bread (save the rest for breakfast). Split open horizontally and turn, cut side down, on a work surface. Press it down hard with the heel of your hand to flatten, then turn right side up. Spread the bottom half with 1 oz (25g) of the butter, then close the bread and cut into two pieces. Wrap in foil and put into a hot oven for at least 15 minutes or until piping hot.

Meanwhile grill the sausages or heat the continental ones in hot (but not boiling) water. Keep warm until the eggs are ready.

When the bread is hot, start the eggs. Beat them lightly with a splash of water and good seasoning of salt and pepper. Melt the remaining butter in a heavy pan and cook the eggs until creamy. Take off the heat quickly and take the bread out of the oven. Remove the foil and fill quickly with the egg and the sausages, cut into thin, lengthwise strips. Press together and eat at once.

Serves 2

🍴 10 minutes   ◉ 15 minutes

Blue Cheese
and Bacon Savoury

For each person:
1 large slice black or granary
  bread
a little butter
1 small stalk celery

1 1/2 oz (40g) Stilton or
  German Blue Brie
1 rasher back bacon

Toast the bread on both sides, then butter one side. Dice the celery and chop the Stilton into small pieces. Grill the bacon until crisp, then crumble.

Put the diced celery, crumbled Stilton and bacon evenly on top of the toast and press down firmly. Place about 3 inches (7.5cm) from a hot grill and leave until bubbly and golden brown.around the edges. Consume at once!

Serves 1

🍴 5 minutes   ◉ 10 minutes

Hot Oscars

4 large frankfurters
2 oz (50g) Cheddar, cut into
 thin strips
4 rashers unsmoked, streaky
 bacon, rind removed

8 oz (225g) puff pastry
a little mustard (optional)
1 small egg, lightly beaten

Split the frankfurters lengthwise down the middle, being careful not to cut all the way through. Stuff the opening with cheese. Stretch the bacon rashers with the back of a knife until almost twice the length of the frankfurters. Then wrap one round each frankfurter and secure with a toothpick or two. Grill the frankfurters until the bacon is almost crisp. Then put to one side.

Roll out the pastry thinly and cut into four large rectangles (slightly longer than the frankfurters and at least three times as wide). Put a frankfurter in the middle of each one and brush with a little mustard (if used), then moisten the edges with a little beaten egg. Roll up and tuck the ends under like a parcel. Turn over, seam side down, and make a series of parallel cuts along the top. Brush lightly with beaten egg and place on a slightly dampened baking tray. Put into a preheated oven (425°F/Gas Mark 7/220°C) and bake for about 20 minutes or until nicely puffed and golden. Eat at once.

Serves 4

🍲 15 minutes   ◉ 5 minutes + 20 minutes (oven)

Devilled Eggs

4 large eggs
3 tablespoons mayonnaise
1 oz (25g) melted butter
2 teaspoons finely chopped
 spring onion

$^1/_2$ teaspoon dry mustard
2 stalks celery, finely diced
salt and pepper

Hard-boil the eggs, then rinse under cold water and peel carefully. Halve the eggs and put the yolks into a small bowl. Blend in the mayonnaise, butter, spring onion, mustard and celery. Season to taste with salt and pepper, then pile back into the egg whites. Dust with finely chopped green tops from the spring onions. Eat with brown bread and butter.

Serves 4

🍲 10 minutes   ◉ 8 minutes

Puddings

The pudding course seems to be alone in defying current trends, becoming rounder and richer all the time. Despite the rise of *nouvelle cuisine*, there has been a glorious revival of good, old-fashioned puds. Yesterday's calorie-conscious are now consuming sticky toffee pudding, treacle sponge and blackcurrant pie without regrets.

The homeliness of puddings seems well suited to suppers, reinforcing all their cosy qualities. If a main course is mainly leftovers, the meal perks up immeasurably with the arrival of a bubbling apple crumble or golden plum cobbler. Crumble mixture can be made in advance, stored in the freezer or fridge and added to the fruit seconds before it goes into the oven. The same applies to cobbler topping, with an egg or milk added at the last minute to bind it all together.

But there are moments (post lasagne or cottage pie) when only a light, icy pud will do. A homemade sorbet or ice-cream, pulled effortlessly from the freezer, solves the problem instantly. If your attempts in the past have produced a granular, snow-like mass, don't despair. The operation is easy, provided you start with a thick fruit purée and an equal quantity of double cream, lightened by beaten egg whites. Rough quantities are: 1/2 pint (275ml) thick fruit purée to 1/2 pint (275ml) lightly whipped double cream to two large egg whites, whisked until stiff with a good pinch of salt. Add a generous squeeze of lemon juice to sharpen the flavour and slightly more sugar than you normally would as the freezing will diminish its strength. Always freeze ice-cream in a plastic container with a lid, in a freezer at its coldest setting. Non-fruit ice-creams will need the addition of custard or beaten egg yolks to keep them creamy. A little boldness at the mixing stage always pays off and combinations like passion fruit and lime, orange and pineapple, coffee and toasted walnut, rum and raisin, mint crisp and chocolate are well worth trying.

Sorbets are a different matter and most need frequent beating during the freezing to prevent ice crystals forming. If you're mad-keen on sorbets, it would be worth investing in a *sorbetière*. These electric wizards do all the hard work, producing a beautifully smooth sorbet while you play.

Last-minute desserts needn't be a toss-up between fresh fruit and something out of a packet or tin. Many of the recipes in this chapter take no more than ten minutes to make. For something light but impressive, try the *ricotta al caffè* (page 104). You can work the same wonders with yogurt. Combine it with puréed fruit and cream cheese or double cream, then layer up with toasted muesli or hazelnuts.

Apple Walnut Crisp

2 lbs (900g) tart dessert apples
3 oz (75g) castor sugar
1/2 teaspoon ground cinnamon

1/2 teaspoon mixed spice
2 tablespoons lemon juice

Crisp Topping
4 oz (100g) plain flour
3 oz (75g) butter
3 oz (75g) soft brown sugar

2 oz (50g) walnut pieces,
    coarsely chopped
1 oz (25g) porridge oats

Peel, quarter and core the apples, then cut into thick slices. Put into a large, deep baking dish and mix in the sugar, spices and lemon juice.

Sift the flour into a large bowl and rub in the butter until it resembles coarse breadcrumbs. Blend in the sugar, chopped walnuts and porridge oats. Scatter this mixture over the apples, making sure it seals the outside edge.

Bake in the centre of a preheated oven (350°F/Gas Mark 4/180°C) for 45–60 minutes or until crisp and nicely browned. Serve warm with natural yogurt or cream.

Serves 6

◗ 15 minutes   ◙ 50 minutes (oven)   ▲▲

98

Quick Apple Crumble

1 1/2 lbs (675g) dessert apples
juice and rind of 1 lemon
4 tablespoons water

3 tablespoons soft brown sugar
light sprinkling of ground
    cinnamon and mixed spice

Crumble Topping
5 oz (150g) plain flour
3 1/2 oz (90g) butter

2 oz (50g) soft brown sugar

Peel and core the apples, then cut into thickish slices. Place in a lightly buttered baking dish (I use a round one, 7 inches/17.5cm in diameter and 2 1/2 inches/3.5cm deep) and pour over the lemon juice and water. Scatter the lemon rind, brown sugar and spices on top.

Sift the flour into a large mixing bowl and rub in the butter. Mix in the brown sugar, then place an even layer of the mixture over the apples.* Place in the centre of a preheated oven (400°F/Gas Mark 6/200°C) and bake for 20 minutes. Then move the dish up a shelf and continue baking for another 20–25 minutes, or until bubbling round the edges and lightly browned on top. Take out and serve warm with cold, thick cream or ice-cream.

Serves 4

◗ 15 minutes   ◙ 40 minutes (oven)   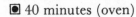 to *

Nanny's Rhubarb Pudding

2 large oranges
1/2 pint (275ml) rhubarb
  purée, about 1/2 lb (225g)
  uncooked weight

a little castor sugar
21/2 oz (65g) demerara sugar

Pudding Top

4 oz (100g) butter, at room
  temperature
4 oz (100g) castor sugar
4 oz (100g) self-raising flour

1/2 teaspoon mixed spice
large pinch of salt
2 standard eggs

Peel and slice the oranges. Sweeten the rhubarb sparingly with castor sugar, then arrange with the oranges in the base of a round, lightly buttered baking dish (7 inches/17.5cm in diameter and 21/2 inches/3.5cm deep is ideal). Scatter the demerara sugar evenly on top.

Cream the butter and sugar together until light. Sift the flour and spice on to a plate or sheet of greaseproof paper. Add a large pinch of salt to the eggs and beat lightly. Add to the creamed mixture alternately with the flour, beating well after each addition. Put large dollops of the batter over the fruit, then smooth out evenly with the back of a spoon. Bake in the centre of a preheated oven (350°F/Gas Mark 4/180°C) for about 45 minutes or until well risen and golden brown. Take out and dust lightly with castor sugar. Serve warm or cold with cream.

Serves 6

� 20 minutes   ◉ 45 minutes (oven)

Lemon Surprise Pudding

A light sponge with creamy lemon sauce beneath.

1 large ripe lemon
1 oz (25g) plain flour
7 oz (200g) castor sugar

1/4 teaspoon salt
2 large eggs, separated
8 fl oz (225ml) milk

Lightly grease 1 round baking dish (about 7 inches/17.5cm in diameter and 21/2 inches/3.5cm deep). Preheat the oven to 350°F/Gas Mark 4/180°C. Grate the lemon rind (being careful to avoid the white pith), then squeeze and strain all the juice. Sift the flour, sugar and salt into a large mixing bowl.

Beat the yolks until thick and lemon-coloured, then blend in the lemon juice and milk. Make a well in the dry ingredients and gradually stir in the egg mixture with the lemon rind.

Whisk the whites until stiff, then lightly fold into the batter. Pour into the baking dish and stand it in a roasting tin filled with about an inch (2.5cm) of warm water. Bake in the centre of the preheated oven for 50 minutes or until lightly browned and firm to the touch. Take out, dust lightly with castor sugar and serve warm.

Serves 6

➚ 20 minutes   ◉ 50 minutes (oven)

Marmalade Bread and Butter Pudding

The best of breakfast in an irresistible pudding.

5 large slices buttered toast from a white sandwich loaf
4 oz (100g) marmalade
2 tablespoons light brown sugar
a little ground cinnamon
3 tablespoons seedless raisins or currants
3 large eggs
3/4 pint (425ml) milk
1 tablespoon whisky or brandy

Remove the crusts from the toast and spread on one side with marmalade. Cut each slice into three equal strips. Butter a small oblong or square baking dish and put a layer of toast, marmalade side up, in the bottom. Sprinkle with a little brown sugar, cinnamon and a few raisins. Repeat the layers until you reach the top of the dish. Beat the eggs, milk and whisky together and pour slowly over the toast. Let stand for 45 minutes* – then bake in a preheated oven (350°F/Gas Mark 4/180°C) for 45 minutes. Take out and serve.

Serves 4

⬤ 15 minutes   Soaking time: 45 minutes   ◙ 45 minutes (oven)   ◖ to *

100

Bananas with Brown Sugar and Rum

Try to make more of this than you need – the leftovers are just as good cold.

2 oz (50g) butter
1 1/2 oz (40g) soft brown sugar
4 large, firm, ripe bananas
juice of 1/2 lemon
sprinkling of ground cinnamon
2 tablespoons white rum

Melt the butter in a large frying or sauté pan. Add the brown sugar and stir until it becomes a smooth syrup. Add the bananas, peeled and halved lengthwise (cut in half again if too big to fit the pan). Cook, basting with the pan juices for a few minutes, then pour over the lemon juice and cinnamon. Continue basting and, when the bananas begin to look slightly translucent (don't let them get mushy), pour over the rum. Flame and remove from the heat. Serve at once, on their own or with vanilla ice-cream.

Serves 4

⬤ 5 minutes   ◙ 7 minutes

Snow Apples

Crisp snowdrifts of meringue with a hot apple centre.

4 medium apples (dessert or cooking)
2 large egg whites

pinch of salt
4 oz (100g) castor sugar

Filling
1 oz (25g) butter
5 tablespoons dried white breadcrumbs
3½ tablespoons orange juice
1½ tablespoons soft brown sugar

1 tablespoon orange marmalade
2 heaped tablespoons raisins or currants

Melt the butter in a small saucepan and blend in the breadcrumbs. Cook until golden and crisp, then add the orange juice, brown sugar and marmalade. Stir until smooth, then blend in the raisins.

Wash the apples and remove the core, taking out a generous centre section. Trim the bottoms so they stand straight, then prick in several places. Fill with the raisin mixture, pressing down well. Stand the apples well apart on a baking tray and bake in a preheated oven (350°F/Gas Mark 4/180°C) for about 40 minutes or until tender.*

Add a pinch of salt to the egg whites and whisk until soft peaks form. Add half the sugar and whisk until stiff and shiny – then fold in the remaining sugar. With a large tablespoon, completely coat each apple with meringue, swirling to make it look like snowdrifts. Put back into the oven and bake for 20–25 minutes or until crisp and golden. Serve warm or cold with cream or yogurt.

Serves 4

🥄 15 minutes   ▣ 10 minutes + 1 hour (oven)   ◖ to *

Prune Whip with Custard Sauce

A favourite nursery pud which seems popular with all ages.

½ lb (225g) large prunes
4 large egg whites
1 teaspoon grated lemon rind

3 tablespoons lemon juice
3 oz (75g) castor sugar

Custard Sauce
1 tablespoon cornflour
2 oz (50g) castor sugar
2 large egg yolks, well beaten

½ pint (275ml) hot milk
few drops vanilla essence

Cook the prunes until soft, then drain completely. Remove the stones and purée the flesh (in a liquidizer or food processor) until smooth.

Put the egg whites, lemon rind, lemon juice and sugar in the top of a double boiler (or in a pyrex bowl over a saucepan of water). Cook over simmering water, beating with an electric whisk, until the mixture becomes light, fluffy and thick enough to hold a soft peak. Remove from the heat and fold in the prune purée. Transfer to a serving dish, cover and chill.

Mix the cornflour and sugar together in a small pudding basin or pyrex bowl. Blend in the egg yolks gradually, then pour the hot milk in slowly. Put over a saucepan of simmering water and cook, stirring frequently, until it is thick enough to coat a metal spoon. Stir in a few drops of vanilla essence, then chill and serve with the prune whip.

Serves 6

🥄 10 minutes   ▣ 45 minutes   ◖

Butterscotch and Banana Cream

1½ oz (40g) butter
4 oz (100g) light brown sugar
4 fl oz (100ml) hot water
10 oz (275g) thick custard
½ pint (275ml) double cream

6–8 large ripe bananas
2 teaspoons lemon juice
2 teaspoons castor sugar
4 oz (100g) wheatmeal
    biscuits, crushed to crumbs

Melt the butter and brown sugar together in a large, heavy frying pan over low heat. When completely melted, bring up to the boil and boil for a minute or two. Then pour in the hot water and stir until completely blended. Reduce the heat and simmer gently until thick and syrupy. Put to one side to cool slightly, then blend in the custard. Whisk the cream until thick and fold in the butterscotch custard.

Slice the bananas into a bowl and sprinkle the lemon juice and castor sugar on top. Mix carefully and leave for 5–10 minutes. Build up layers of bananas, butterscotch cream and biscuit crumbs in a large glass bowl, ending with a layer of crumbs. Decorate the top if you like, just before serving, with a little piped whipped cream and additional banana slices.

Serves 6–8

🥣 10–15 minutes   ◉ 10 minutes   ✱

Summer Pudding

This is at its best if left to soak for a full twenty-four hours before serving.

1½ lb (675g) fresh raspberries
½ lb (225g) blackberries or
    blackcurrants
4 oz (100g) castor sugar

a little lemon juice
7–8 thin slices of good white
    bread, crusts removed

Rinse the fruits lightly, drain well, then put into a large, heavy saucepan. Add the sugar and a squeeze of lemon juice and cook for 3–4 minutes, until the juices begin to run and the sugar has dissolved. Take off the heat and taste, adding more sugar or lemon juice if required.

Line a 1½ pint (850ml) pudding basin with bread slices, making sure there are no gaps, and pour in the fruit and its juices, reserving about half a cupful. Cover the top with the remaining slices and put a plate on top. Put a weight (a bag of sugar would do) on top and chill overnight. Turn out, coat with the remaining fruit and juices and serve with lightly whipped cream. (If you have a sudden urge to make this in mid-winter, use frozen raspberries and blackberries – making sure they are completely thawed first. If you have to resort to tinned fruit, drain all of the juice first and adjust the sugar accordingly.)

Serves 4–6

🥣 10 minutes   ◉ 4 minutes   Chilling time: overnight
◑ ✱

Toffee Apples with Yogurt

1 oz (25g) butter
4 level tablespoons golden syrup
2 tablespoons light brown sugar
2 lbs (900g) firm dessert apples
2 tablespoons lemon juice
1/4 pint (150ml) double cream
2 5-oz (150g) tubs natural yogurt
1/2 teaspoon ground cinnamon
1 tablespoon castor sugar

Melt the butter in a large, heavy frying pan, then add the syrup and sugar. Stir over low heat until well blended, then slowly bring up to the boil. Simmer gently until the mixture becomes a light toffee colour.

While the sugar mixture is caramelizing, peel, core and slice the apples into quarters or eighths (depending on their size). As soon as the caramel is ready, add the apple slices to the pan (you'll have to do this in several lots as the apples will bruise if you overcrowd the pan). Baste them with the caramel and cook, turning them once, until just soft and translucent. Lift out carefully and put into a bowl. When all the apples have been cooked, pour the lemon juice over them and any toffee mixture remaining in the pan (scrape this out with a spatula).

Whisk the cream until thick, then whisk in the yogurt, cinnamon and sugar. Build up layers of apple slices (with a spoonful of their juice) and cream in wine glasses, ending with a layer of cream and a single apple slice to decorate. Chill well before serving.

Serves 6

 10 minutes   20 minutes

Spiced Caramel Oranges

5 oz (150g) castor sugar
4 fl oz (100ml) water
2 fl oz (50ml) lemon juice
1/4 teaspoon ground ginger
1/4 teaspoon ground cinnamon
6 large oranges

Place the sugar in a large, heavy pan and melt over moderate heat, stirring occasionally with a wooden spoon, until it turns a rich caramel colour. Take off the heat and pour in the water (stand back as it will hiss furiously). Stir over gentle heat until the caramel has melted and the mixture is thoroughly blended. Mix in the lemon juice and the spices, then remove from the heat.

As you wait for the sugar to melt, peel the oranges, taking care to remove all the white pith. Cut into horizontal slices, then place in a bowl. Pour over the caramel sauce and leave for 1–2 hours, basting with the juice whenever you think of it.

Serves 4

 10 minutes   20 minutes

Holly Berry Salad

With its striking colours, this makes a refreshing winter fruit salad.

3 oz (75g) granulated sugar
6 fl oz (175ml) water
juice of 1 large ripe lemon, strained
1/2 lb (225g) seedless green grapes

1/2 large ripe honeydew melon
2 crisp green-skinned apples
1–2 tablespoons brandy
1/2 lb (225g) frozen raspberries, thawed
2 kiwi fruit, peeled and sliced

Heat the sugar, water and lemon juice in a heavy saucepan. When the sugar has dissolved, bring up rapidly to the boil and cook until it becomes syrupy. Remove from the heat and allow to cool.

When the syrup is cold, prepare the fruit. Halve the grapes (or leave whole if small). Scoop out the flesh from the melon and cut into medium chunks. Quarter, core and cut the apples into medium chunks. Put these three fruits into a glass bowl and pour over the syrup and brandy. Toss until well coated, then carefully fold in the raspberries and half the kiwi fruit. Arrange the remaining kiwi on top, cover the bowl with cling-film and chill for at least 30 minutes (but no longer than several hours, otherwise the fruit will become mushy).

Serves 6–8

🍮 15 minutes　◼ 10 minutes　Chilling time: 30 minutes

104

Ricotta al Caffè

Demoralizingly delicious, and only takes a minute to make.

1 lb (450g) ricotta cheese
3 oz (75g) sifted icing sugar
2 level tablespoons instant coffee powder

3–4 tablespoons white rum
1/4 pint (150ml) double cream
chocolate shavings (optional)

In a large bowl (or in a food processor or liquidizer), whisk the ricotta until smooth. Blend in the sifted icing sugar, coffee powder and then the rum. Whisk the cream until just thick, then fold into the ricotta mixture. Cover and chill for at least 1 hour. (This will come to no harm if made the day before it is needed.)

When ready to serve, divide the mixture between glasses or ramekin dishes. Top with a light dusting of coffee powder or chocolate shavings. Serve with crisp biscuits (if you have them).

Serves 4–6

🍮 10 minutes　Chilling time: 1 hour

Good Golly, Miss Molly

I've long forgotten how this pudding got its name, but its taste is unforgettable.

6 fl oz (175ml) double cream
1½ teaspoons Camp coffee
    essence
1½ tablespoons castor sugar
1½ tablespoons brandy
2 5-oz (150g) packets
    Gingerella biscuits

Whisk the cream until just thick, then add the coffee essence, castor sugar and brandy. Whisk again until thick, taking care not to overdo it (it should be thick enough to stay on the biscuits but not so thick that it becomes buttery).

Take a Gingerella biscuit, spread with a thin layer of coffee cream and stand – cream side up – on a large plate. Continue like this until you have two stacks, each about 12 biscuits high. Carefully put the stacks end to end on the plate to make one long, tube-like log. Use the remaining cream to ice the sides and ends of the roll (if you use a round-ended knife, you can make it look like bark). Don't overwork the cream or it will lose its creaminess. Cover loosely with foil and refrigerate for at least an hour. It's at its best 1–2 hours after making. When ready to serve, cut the roll diagonally into medium slices.

Serves 6

10 minutes   Chilling time: 1 hour

Highland Cream

4 oz (100g) thick honey
4½ tablespoons whisky
1 tablespoon lemon juice
½ pint (275ml) double cream
4–6 tablespoons toasted fine
    oatmeal

Put the honey into a saucepan with the whisky and lemon juice. Heat gently, stirring all the time, until the honey melts and the mixture is smooth. Take off the heat and cool.

Whisk the cream until thick, then fold in the honey mixture and whisk again until thick. Chill until needed, then divide between thin wine glasses and top with toasted oatmeal. (If raspberries are in season, you could layer them with the cream in the glasses.)

Serves 4

10 minutes   ✱

Bitter Chocolate Mousse

4 oz (100g) dark chocolate, unsweetened
2 tablespoons undiluted frozen orange juice, thawed
2 teaspoons Camp coffee essence
2 tablespoons brandy (optional)
1/2 pint (275ml) double cream
2 large egg whites
pinch of salt

Chop up the chocolate roughly and put into a pyrex bowl and over a saucepan of barely simmering water. When completely melted, remove from the heat and gradually stir in the orange juice, coffee essence and brandy.

Allow to cool slightly, then whisk the cream until thick. Fold into the chocolate mixture. Whisk the egg whites with a pinch of salt until stiff, then fold lightly into the other ingredients. Transfer to ramekin dishes and chill for an hour or so before serving. (This, if frozen, makes a very creamy chocolate ice-cream but should be eaten within three days – otherwise the texture will deteriorate.)

Serves 6

⬩ about 10–15 minutes ◉ 10 minutes Chilling time: 1 hour ◐ ▲▲

106

The Mars Mousse

3 Mars bars
3 tablespoons strong hot coffee
1 large egg yolk
1/2 pint (275ml) double cream
2 level tablespoons castor sugar (scant 1 oz/25g)
2 large egg whites
pinch of salt

Chop the Mars bars up roughly and put into a pyrex bowl over a saucepan of barely simmering water. Leave until completely melted (don't stir, but press the mixture occasionally with the tip of a wooden spoon to see how far it has melted). Take off the heat and gradually blend in the hot coffee.

Allow to cool slightly, then blend in the egg yolk. Whisk the cream until thick, then fold lightly into the Mars mixture. Whisk the egg whites with a pinch of salt until soft peaks form. Fold in the sugar and continue whisking until stiff. Fold lightly into the other ingredients. Transfer to small ramekin dishes, cover with foil or cling-film and freeze. (It will never freeze solid so you only need to allow a few minutes for it to 'come to' and then it's ready to eat.)

Serves 6

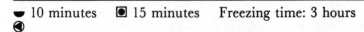

⬩ 10 minutes ◉ 15 minutes Freezing time: 3 hours ◐

Brown Bread Ice-cream

2 large, thick slices of granary bread	4 large eggs
1½ rounded tablespoons demerara sugar	¾ pint (425ml) double cream
	pinch of salt
	3½ oz (90g) sifted icing sugar

Preheat the oven to 350°F/Gas Mark 4/180°C. Pull the bread into small pieces and place close together on a shallow baking tray. Sprinkle the demerara sugar evenly over the top and put the tray into the oven. Bake for about 1 hour or until the sugar has caramelized slightly and the bread is crisp and lightly browned. Cool, then tip the contents of the tray into a polythene bag and, using a rolling pin, crush to coarse crumbs (it gives a crunchier texture to the ice-cream if the crumbs are not too fine).

Separate the eggs. Whisk the cream until just thick, then whisk in the egg yolks (being careful not to let the mixture get too thick). Add a pinch of salt to the egg whites and whisk until just stiff, then whisk in half the icing sugar. Fold in the remainder carefully. Sprinkle the crumbs and demerara sugar over the cream mixture, add the egg whites and fold in lightly. Transfer to a large plastic container, cover with a lid and freeze until firm.

Serves 8

◗ 20 minutes   ◉ 1 hour   Freezing time: 3 hours   ◖

Blackberry and Lemon Ice-cream

6 oz (175g) granulated sugar	1 large ripe lemon
4 fl oz (100ml) water	½ pint (275ml) double cream
8 oz (225g) blackberries, fresh or frozen	

Put the sugar and water into a saucepan and heat gently until the sugar has dissolved, stirring occasionally. Add the blackberries (if using frozen, make sure they're completely thawed first) and cook until thick and pulpy. Take off the heat and leave to cool.

Squeeze and strain all the lemon juice and add to the blackberries. Whisk the cream until just thick and fold in lightly. Pour into a plastic container, cover with a lid and freeze until firm.

Serves 6–8

◗ 15 minutes   ◉ 20 minutes   Freezing time: 3 hours
◖

Pies, Cakes, Biscuits and Breads

This chapter is, by nature, impossible to finish. It is a subject which provokes such unbridled enthusiasm that attempts to restrain it are quite hopeless. Like compiling the year's best books or films, everyone's shortlist is different – each longer than the one before it.

The pudding chapter is practical, composed mainly of recipes which can be made in ten minutes or the day before. This one is pure indulgence – the recipes that no one could resist. Take, for instance, the passion cake. Foolishly, I had thought that any cake with oil in it could only be revolting. Quite the opposite. It is feather-light, with a wonderful, nutty flavour – superbly matched by its cream cheese icing.

English cooks, seduced on holiday by the delectable *tarte tatin*, rush home to reproduce it in the comfort of their own kitchens, only to find that the instructions for its manufacture are maddeningly diverse. Should you bake it in a pie dish, a cake tin, make the caramel beforehand, brown it after, serve it warm, leave it cold – *mon Dieu*, it's confusing. After a prolonged session at the stove, I can now offer the definitive version – golden, caramelized apples resting happily on a crisp pastry base.

An equal favourite is the Banoffi pie, made famous by the Hungry Monk Restaurant in Jevington, East Sussex. It is a combination so inspired, so devastatingly good that few people can guess the ingredients – or fail to ask for a second helping. Just as irresistible is the rhubarb meringue pie on page 109. The sourness of the fruit makes a perfect foil for the sweet meringue.

While bread-making is easy and therapeutic, it often becomes an infrequent pleasure because it *does* take time. The granary bread on page 113 is a good compromise. It only needs one rising and, if left in an airing cupboard to prove, takes just under 1½ hours to make.

Soda breads and scones take even less time and are perfect companions for homemade soup. When making a free-standing soda bread, follow the advice given by Elizabeth David in her classic *English Bread and Yeast Cookery* and cover it with an inverted cake tin as it bakes. This creates a steamy atmosphere which, in turn, produces a light, moist bread with a crisp crust.

Quick breads and biscuits are such a useful stopgap that several are given at the end of the chapter. Wholemeal banana bread and butterscotch brownies are so popular that it's a positive advantage to have them within easy reach.

Rhubarb Meringue Pie

6 oz (175g) sweet shortcrust
  pastry
1 egg white, lightly beaten
3 large egg whites

¼ teaspoon cream of tartar
large pinch of salt
6 oz (175g) castor sugar

Filling
3 large egg yolks
4 oz (100g) castor sugar
2 level tablespoons flour
1 oz (25g) unsalted butter,
  melted and cooled

large pinch of salt
1 lb (450g) rhubarb, trimmed
  and diced

Roll out the pastry, then use to line a 9-inch, deep pie plate or flan ring. Prick the bottom lightly, line with greaseproof paper and fill with baking beans. Bake in a preheated oven (425°F/Gas Mark 7/220°C) for 12–15 minutes. Remove the paper and beans and brush the bottom and sides with a little egg white. Bake for a further 5–7 minutes.

As it bakes, put the egg yolks and sugar into a large bowl and beat with an electric whisk until thick and lemon-coloured. Whisk in the flour, butter and salt. Fold in the rhubarb and transfer the mixture to the pastry shell. Bake in a preheated oven (375°F/Gas Mark 5/190°C) for 35–45 minutes. Cool slightly.

Beat the egg whites with the cream of tartar and salt until they hold soft peaks. Whisk in the sugar gradually and continue whisking until stiff. Spread over the pie, swirling with a spatula. Bake in a cool oven (300°F/Gas Mark 2/150°C) until the meringue is lightly browned. Cool on a wire rack and serve when cold.

Serves 8

☛ 30 minutes   ◙ 1½ hours (oven)   Cooling time: 30 minutes   ◐

Tarte Tatin

3 oz (75g) unsalted butter
6 tablespoons castor sugar
2 lbs (900g) dessert apples
ground cinnamon

ground mixed spice
5 oz (175g) sweet shortcrust
  pastry

Melt 2 oz (50g) of the butter in an 8-inch (20cm) cake tin (at least 1 inch/2.5cm deep and preferably non-stick) on top of the stove, over very low heat. Blend in 4 tablespoons of the sugar, then leave, shaking the tin occasionally, until it has turned a rich caramel colour. Take off the heat.

Peel, quarter and core the apples, then slice thinly. Arrange a bottom layer of apple slices in the tin, in overlapping circles (remembering that this will be the top when turned out). Place another layer on top and sprinkle with a little ground cinnamon, mixed spice and a tablespoon of sugar. Repeat with the remaining apples, then melt the remaining butter and drizzle on top. Put a tight-fitting lid (or foil) on the tin, then place over a gentle heat. Cook for 15 minutes, then remove the lid and cook for 15–20 minutes, until the liquid (when the tin is tipped to one side) looks syrupy. Cool completely.

Roll out the pastry to fit the top of the tin. Place on top of the apples and let the sides drop down inside the tin. Make a few short slits in the top, then bake in a preheated oven (375°F/Gas Mark 5/190°C), on the second shelf from the top, for about 30 minutes – or until the pastry is golden brown. Cool to lukewarm (or serve cold), then reverse carefully on to a plate.

Serves 6–8

☛ 15–20 minutes   ◙ 45 minutes + 30 minutes (oven)   Cooling time: 1 hour   ◐

Banoffi Pie

The creation of the Hungry Monk Restaurant, its secret will confound even the most sophisticated palate.

1 14-oz (397g) tin sweetened condensed milk
6 oz (175g) sweet shortcrust pastry
1/2 pint (275ml) double cream

1 rounded teaspoon powdered instant coffee
1 oz (25g) castor sugar
1 large banana, peeled and chopped

The secret of this delicious pie lies in the condensed milk. Immerse the can *unopened* in boiling water. Cover and boil for 4 hours, topping up the water from time to time. Remove from the water and allow to cool completely before opening. Inside you will find the soft toffee filling.

Butter the inside of an 8-inch (20cm) flan ring or tin and line with a thin layer of shortcrust pastry. Bake blind for about 25 minutes or until crisp and golden. Allow to cool.

Whisk the cream with the coffee and sugar until thick. Then scrape out the toffee mixture into the flan case and spread evenly with the back of a spoon. Put the banana in an even layer on top. Finish by spooning or piping on the cream.

Serves 8

🥄 20 minutes ◼ 4 hours + 25 minutes (oven) ◀

110

French Lemon Tart

6 oz (175g) sweet shortcrust pastry
2 large eggs
4 oz (100g) castor sugar
rind and juice of 2 large lemons (2–3 fl oz/50–75ml juice)

4 fl oz (100ml) double cream
a little icing sugar

Line an 8-inch (20cm) flan ring or tin with pastry, prick the base lightly with a fork and bake blind for 17–20 minutes (removing the paper and beans after 12 minutes).

As the pastry bakes, prepare the filling. Beat the eggs and sugar with an electric whisk until very pale and thick (when the whisk is lifted out, it should leave a trail behind). Mix in the lemon juice and rind, then whisk the cream until just thick and fold in lightly.

Ladle the mixture into the tart shell and bake at 375°F/Gas Mark 5/190°C for 20–30 minutes or until puffed and golden. Take out and dust lightly with icing sugar. Serve warm or cold.

Serves 6

🥄 20 minutes ◼ 45 minutes (oven)

Dorset Apple Cake

4 oz (100g) butter
1 medium egg
4 oz (100g) castor sugar
1/2 lb (225g) self-raising flour
3/4 lb (350g) dessert apples
2 oz (50g) raisins

1/2 level teaspoon mixed spice
1/2 level teaspoon ground cinnamon
1 tablespoon sugar
a little lemon juice
castor or icing sugar to finish

Preheat the oven to 350°F/Gas Mark 4/180°C. Melt the butter, then scrape out into a large mixing bowl. Lightly beat the egg and blend into the butter with the sugar. Sift the flour and mix in gradually. Place half this mixture in the bottom of a deep, round 8-inch (20cm) cake tin, greased and lightly dusted with flour.

Peel, core and roughly chop the apples. Put in a bowl with the raisins, spices, sugar and a good squeeze of lemon juice. Mix well, then arrange the apple mixture in an even layer on top of the dough in the tin. Then cover with the remaining dough, pressing out evenly with your fingers.

Put the tin into the centre of the preheated oven and bake for about an hour, or until the top is golden brown. Take out, loosen round the edges with a knife and carefully reverse out on to a wire rack. Turn right side up and dust lightly with castor or sifted icing sugar. Serve warm or cold, on its own or with lightly whipped cream.

Serves 6–8

◖ 20 minutes   ◉ 1 hour   ◀   ▲▲

Dutch Plum Cake

6 oz (175g) self-raising flour
1 level teaspoon baking powder
large pinch of salt
1/2 level teaspoon cinnamon

4 oz (100g) castor sugar
grated rind of 1 large orange
1 oz (25g) melted butter
3 fl oz (75ml) milk
1 large egg, lightly beaten

Topping
1 oz (25g) butter
1 1/2 lb (675g) fresh plums or peaches, or tinned, drained

3 oz (75g) castor sugar
1 level teaspoon ground cinnamon

Preheat the oven to 350°F/Gas Mark 4/180°C and grease a shallow baking tin, 11 inches (27.5cm) × 7 inches (17.5cm).

Sift the flour, baking powder, salt and cinnamon into a large mixing bowl. Blend in the sugar and orange rind. Make a well in the centre, then pour in the butter, milk and egg. Blend quickly to make a smooth batter. Spread out evenly in the prepared tin.

Melt the topping butter and brush lightly over the batter. Remove the plums' stones and slice thinly lengthwise. Arrange in rows, overlapping them slightly, on top of the batter. Mix the castor sugar and cinnamon together and sprinkle evenly on top.

Bake in the centre of the oven for 35–40 minutes. Take out and loosen gently round the outside edges with a knife, then cool slightly and cut into squares. Lift out with a palette knife (or cool completely in the tin and lift the squares out later).

Serves 6

◖ 20 minutes   ◉ 40 minutes (oven)   ◀

Passion Cake

Carrot cake – with feeling.

4 large eggs	2 level teaspoons bicarbonate
6 oz (175g) soft brown sugar	of soda
3 oz (75g) thick honey	1/2 teaspoon salt
8 fl oz (225ml) corn oil	4 oz (100g) chopped walnuts
9 oz (250g) plain flour	or pecans
1 level teaspoon cinnamon	10 oz (275g) grated carrots

Cream Cheese Icing

6 oz (175g) cream cheese	5 oz (150g) sifted icing sugar
2 oz (50g) unsalted butter, at	1 teaspoon lemon juice
room temperature	few drops of vanilla essence

Preheat the oven to 350°F/Gas Mark 4/180°C. Put the eggs, sugar and honey into a large mixing bowl and beat with an electric whisk until light. Beat in the oil gradually. Sift the flour, cinnamon, soda and salt on to a plate, then gradually blend in with the walnuts and carrots.

Grease and lightly flour two 8-inch (20cm) cake tins (at least 1 inch/2.5cm deep). Divide the batter evenly between them and bake (switching them round halfway through if you have to put them on two shelves) for 35–45 minutes or until a toothpick inserted in the centre comes out clean. Cool for 5 minutes, then loosen round the edges, reverse out on to a rack and stand right side up. Cool completely.

Put the cream cheese and butter into a mixing bowl. Whisk until light, then gradually beat in the icing sugar, lemon juice and vanilla. Spread just under half the icing on one cake, place the other one on top and cover with the remaining icing.

Serves 10

⏷ 30 minutes   ◙ 40 minutes (oven)

Butterscotch Brownies

2 oz (50g) butter	1 level teaspoon baking
6 oz (175g) soft brown sugar	powder
1 egg, lightly beaten with a	1/4 teaspoon salt
pinch of salt	2 oz (50g) finely chopped
1/2 teaspoon vanilla essence	walnuts
4 oz (100g) plain flour	

Preheat the oven to 350°F/Gas Mark 4/180°C. Grease an 8-inch (20cm) square tin.

Melt the butter in a medium saucepan over low heat and stir in the brown sugar. Cool slightly, then stir in the lightly beaten egg and the vanilla. Sift the flour, baking powder and salt together and gradually blend into the sugar mixture. Fold in the chopped walnuts. Scrape the butter into the prepared tin and level off with the back of a spoon. Bake just above the centre of the oven for 20–25 minutes (if a toothpick inserted in the centre comes out clean, it is ready). Take out, mark into squares or fingers and cool slightly before removing from the tin (or cool completely in the tin and take out later). When cold, store in a polythene bag or wrap in cling-film.

Makes about 16 squares

⏷ 15 minutes   ◙ 25 minutes (oven)

Wholemeal Banana Bread

3 ripe medium bananas
2 large eggs
pinch of salt
1 oz (25g) butter
3 tablespoons thick honey
1/2 teaspoon vanilla essence
1 tablespoon lemon juice
1/2 lb (225g) plain flour
5 oz (150g) soft brown sugar

1 level teaspoon bicarbonate of
  soda
1 level teaspoon baking
  powder
1/2 teaspoon salt
11/2 oz (40g) bran
3 oz (75g) finely chopped
  walnuts

Preheat the oven to 350°F/Gas Mark 4/180°F. Grease a 2-lb (900g) loaf tin.

Put the bananas into a medium bowl and mash until very mushy. Beat the eggs with a pinch of salt until light and blend into the bananas. Melt the butter with the honey over gentle heat. When thoroughly blended, take off the heat and stir in the vanilla and lemon juice. Mix into the bananas.

Sift the flour, sugar, soda, baking powder and salt into a large mixing bowl. Mix in the bran and chopped walnuts. Make a well in the centre, pour in the liquid ingredients and mix, with a wooden spoon, only until all the flour has been incorporated (don't overmix or the texture of the bread will be spoiled). Transfer to the prepared tin, level off with the back of a spoon and bake for 1 hour. (If a toothpick inserted in the centre comes out clean, it is ready.) Take out, loosen around the sides with a round-topped knife and carefully reverse out on to a wire rack. Stand right side up and leave to cool. When cold, store in a polythene bag (it will keep for almost a week if properly stored).

Makes 1 large loaf

🥄 15 minutes   ◉ 1 hour (oven)   ◑   ▲▲

Easy Granary Bread

2 level teaspoons dried yeast
1 teaspoon brown sugar
5 fl oz (150ml) hand-hot water
1/2 lb (225g) granary flour
1/2 lb (225g) wholewheat flour

1 teaspoon salt
1 oz (25g) butter
5–6 fl oz (150–175ml)
  hand-hot water

Grease a 2-lb (900g) bread tin or two 1-lb (450g) tins. Mix the dried yeast and brown sugar with 5 fl oz (150ml) of hand-hot water. Leave in a warm place for 15 minutes or until frothy.

Blend the flours and salt together, then rub in the butter. Make a well in the centre, then pour in the yeast mixture with an additional 5 fl oz (150ml) of hand-hot water. Mix until you have a firm dough, adding the remaining water if needed. Knead until smooth and elastic (3–5 minutes), then put into the greased tin, pressing well into the corners. Cover with a cloth or cling-film and leave in a warm place until the dough has risen to the top of the tin. When it gets near the top, preheat the oven to 400°F/Gas Mark 6/200°C.

Remove the cloth, brush the top of the dough lightly with milk and bake in the centre of the oven for about 30 minutes, or until nicely browned. Loosen round the edges of the tin with a knife, then reverse out. If the bottom of the loaf doesn't sound hollow when rapped with your knuckles, return to the oven for 5–10 more minutes. Cool on a wire rack, then store in a polythene bag.

Makes 1 large loaf or 2 smaller ones

🥄 20 minutes   Rising time: 40 minutes   ◉ 30 minutes (oven)   ◑

Wholemeal Celery and Cheese Scones

3 oz (75g) butter
4 oz (100g) finely chopped onion
2 large stalks celery, finely diced
4 oz (100g) wholewheat flour
4 oz (100g) plain flour
1 teaspoon bicarbonate of soda
2 teaspoons cream of tartar
1/4 teaspoon salt
several twists of black pepper
4 oz (100g) good Cheddar, grated
1 large egg, lightly beaten
2–3 fl oz (50–75ml) milk

Preheat the oven to 425°F/Gas Mark 7/220°C. Grease and generously dust a large baking tray with wholewheat flour.

Melt 1 oz (25g) of butter in a medium pan. Add the onion and celery and cook slowly until the onion is pale golden, the celery just soft. Lift out and put to one side.

Sift the flours, soda, cream of tartar, salt and pepper into a large mixing bowl, tipping in the bran that remains in the sieve. Rub in the remaining butter until the mixture resembles coarse breadcrumbs. Blend in the onion and celery mixture (with its buttery juices) and the cheese, then make a well in the middle. Pour in the egg with half the milk. Mix to a soft dough, adding more milk if necessary. Turn out on to a lightly floured surface and knead lightly until smooth. Roll out to a 3/4-inch (.75cm) thickness and cut into rounds. Place on the baking tray and brush the tops lightly with milk. Bake in the preheated oven for 20 minutes or until well risen and a rich, golden brown. Serve warm with butter (or leave to cool on a wire rack, store in a polythene bag and reheat when needed).

Makes 10 large scones

🌣 25 minutes ▣ 15 minutes + 20 minutes (oven) ◑ ▲▲

114

Quick Irish Soda Bread

If no buttermilk is available, use half milk, half water and 2 teaspoons of cream of tartar with the soda.

1 1/2 lbs (675g) wholemeal flour
1/4 lb (100g) strong white flour
2 teaspoons bicarbonate of soda
1 teaspoon salt
1 pint (575ml) buttermilk (scant)

Grease two 1-lb (225g) loaf tins (or one 2-lb/900g tin) and dust lightly with flour. Preheat the oven to 425°F/Gas Mark 7/220°C.

Sift the flours, soda and salt into a large mixing bowl, tipping in at the end the bran that remains. Make a well in the centre and pour in almost all the buttermilk. Mix to a stiff but not sticky dough, adding more buttermilk if necessary.

Turn the dough out on to a lightly floured work surface and knead for several minutes. Then divide in two and press each half into a loaf tin. Level off the top and press the dough well into the corners. Bake in the preheated oven for 25–30 minutes, then remove the loaves from their tins and return them to the oven for a further 10–15 minutes. (The bread is ready when the bottom of the loaf sounds hollow when tapped.)

Makes 1 large or 2 small loaves

🌣 15 minutes ▣ 40–50 minutes

Storecupboard Cooking

As some of the best suppers are the result of improvisation, it pays to have a well-stocked larder or freezer. The list below gives a generous guide to what these might contain – and all the recipes in this chapter can be made from items on it.

Supper-making becomes effortless once you get rid of the last-minute 'fiddles'. For instance, grating cheese: instead of doing this when you need it, grate a large 2-lb (900g) wedge at one time. Divide into bags of 4 oz (100g) and put several in the refrigerator, the rest in the freezer. Then it is simply a matter of reaching for it – with no measuring or grating. Do the same with breadcrumbs, croûtons, chopped walnuts, parsley and other herbs.

STORECUPBOARD BASICS

Dairy
long-life milk
long-life single and whipping
  cream

eggs
Parmesan cheese
wedge of Cheddar

Wet
olive and vegetable oil
wine vinegar
Worcestershire sauce
soy sauce
tomato ketchup

mango chutney
mayonnaise
mustard
marmalade
apricot jam/redcurrant jelly

Dry
English mustard
chicken and beef stock cubes
plain and brown sugar
dried yeast
baking powder/bicarbonate of
  soda/cream of tartar
spices
raisins
pasta
herbs

plain and self-raising flour
wholewheat flour
crunchy oat cereal
rice
pulses
lemons
onions
garlic
potatoes

Tins
sweetcorn
ham
mushrooms
peas
soups
Italian tomatoes
tuna/salmon/sardines
anchovies/prawns

asparagus pieces
tomato sauce
baked beans
cannellini beans
apricots/peaches/blackberries
tomato purée
molasses/treacle

In the freezer
bread
butter
grated cheese
breadcrumbs
chicken pieces
minced beef/lamb/pork

prawns
spinach
beans/peas
bacon
frankfurters
pastry

115

Tomato and Basil Tarts

6 oz (175g) shortcrust pastry

Filling

1 oz (25g) butter	1 tablespoon wine or water
1 small onion, peeled and finely chopped	pinch of sugar
1 14-oz (400g) tin Italian tomatoes	1 level teaspoon dried basil
1 level tablespoon tomato purée	salt and pepper

Roll out the pastry and use to line a Yorkshire pudding tin (or 4 large tartlet tins), well greased. Prick the bottoms lightly with a fork, line with greaseproof paper and beans. Bake in a hot oven (425°F/Gas Mark 7/220°C) for 10 minutes, then remove the paper and beans and bake for a further 5–7 minutes. Take out and put to one side.

Meanwhile, heat the butter in a heavy saucepan and sauté the onion until pale golden. Add the tomatoes and their juice, breaking them up with a wooden spoon. Add the tomato purée, water or wine, sugar, basil (crumbling it to release the flavour) with a good seasoning of salt and black pepper. Cook over a low heat, stirring frequently, for 5–8 minutes or until it becomes a thickish (but not dry) purée.

Divide the mixture between the pastry cases, filling them generously as it will shrink slightly as it cooks. Scatter a little more chopped basil on top and bake on the second shelf from the top of the oven (375°F/Gas Mark 5/190°C) for about 20 minutes, until the pastry is nicely browned and the filling piping hot. Take out and serve.

Serves 4, or 2 ravenous eaters

🥄10 minutes ◼ 5–8 minutes + 40 minutes (oven) ◐ ▲▲

116

Boston Baked Beans (Quick Method)

4 oz (100g) salt pork (failing that, streaky bacon)	2 tablespoons tomato purée
2 tablespoons bacon fat *or* 1 oz (25g) butter	1 pint (575ml) water
	2 teaspoons French mustard
4 oz (100g) chopped onion	1 tablespoon dark brown sugar
2 stalks celery, diced	1 teaspoon wine or cider vinegar
2 14-oz (400g) tins haricot or Italian cannellini beans, drained	salt and pepper
	4 frankfurters *or* 2 extra large ones
3 level tablespoons molasses or black treacle	

Remove the tough outer skin from the salt pork, then cut into thin strips. Melt half the bacon fat or butter in a large, flameproof casserole and toss the salt pork in it. Cook over a moderate heat until the pork has darkened in colour and browned lightly. Add the remaining fat and cook the onion and celery until slightly softened.

Add the cannellini beans (well drained and rinsed under cold water), molasses, tomato purée, water, mustard, sugar and vinegar. Give a good seasoning of salt and pepper, then bring up to a gentle simmer. Cover and continue simmering for 30 minutes, then partly covered for a further 30 minutes. Cut the frankfurters into diagonal slices and add to the pot. Cook for a final 15 minutes, then taste and adjust the seasoning if necessary. Keep warm until needed (or cool and reheat when needed).

Serves 4–6

🥄 15 minutes ◼ 1½ hours

Spaghetti with Egg and Bacon Sauce

The secret of a good carbonara *is to use only the yolks. (Not as wasteful as it sounds when the whites can make a refreshing sorbet to follow.)*

1 lb (450g) spaghetti or linguine   salt

Sauce

1 oz (25g) butter
1 small onion, peeled and finely chopped (about 4 oz/100g)
6 rashers back bacon, finely diced

4 large egg yolks
3–4 tablespoons freshly grated Parmesan
salt and black pepper
chopped parsley
extra Parmesan to serve

Fill a large pot with water, cover and bring to the boil.

As you wait for the water, begin the sauce. Melt the butter in a heavy, medium pan and add the chopped onion. Cook until golden, then add the bacon dice. Continue cooking, stirring occasionally, until crisp. Keep warm until the pasta is ready.

When the water has come to a rolling boil, add a handful of salt and the pasta. Stir as it returns to the boil, then cook uncovered until it is *al dente*. (Do test frequently – it mustn't lose its 'bite'.) Drain in a large colander, then tip into the pan with the onion and bacon. Beat the yolks lightly with a fork, then pour over the pasta. Mix quickly, over a low heat, until the egg yolks thicken and give a golden coating to the pasta. Mix in about 3 tablespoons of Parmesan and a good seasoning of salt and black pepper. Transfer to a hot dish, dust with parsley and serve with extra Parmesan.

Serves 4

🥄 10 minutes   ◉ 15 minutes   ✱

SC – H✱

Beano's Beef Casserole

8 oz (225g) short macaroni
salt
pepper
12 oz (350g) finely chopped onion
1¹/₂ oz (40g) butter
1 lb (450g) lean minced beef
1 15-oz (425g) tin mushrooms well drained
6 oz (175g) good Cheddar, grated

1 12-oz (350ml) tin cream of tomato soup
1 level tablespoon tomato purée
8 fl oz (225ml) milk
1¹/₂ tablespoons Worcestershire sauce
1 teaspoon sugar
4 tablespoons dried breadcrumbs
1 oz (25g) melted butter

Start by cooking the macaroni in plenty of salted boiling water until *al dente*, then tip into a colander and rinse under warm running water. Season well with salt and pepper, then put to one side.

As the macaroni cooks, sauté the onion in the butter (in a very large sauté or frying pan) until golden. Push to one side of the pan and add the meat. Brown quickly, then skim off any excess fat. Add the mushrooms, cheese, tomato soup, tomato purée, milk, Worcestershire sauce and sugar. Stir over gentle heat until well blended, then season to taste with salt and pepper. Mix in the macaroni, then transfer to a large, deep baking dish. Scatter the breadcrumbs on top, then pour over the melted butter evenly.* Bake in a preheated oven (350°F/Gas Mark 4/180°F) for 30–40 minutes or until bubbling round the edges and piping hot.

Serves 6–8

🥄 10 minutes   ◉ 15 minutes + 35 minutes (oven)
◖ to *   ▲▲

117

Creamed Salmon Croustades

4 thick slices of wholemeal
  bread
1 oz (25g) melted butter
1½ oz (65g) butter
1½ oz (40g) flour
¾ pint (350ml) milk
1 7-oz (200g) tin red or pink
  salmon, juice drained but
  reserved

1 tablespoon finely chopped
  parsley
4 oz (100g) cooked peas
2 large hard-boiled eggs,
  quartered
a little lemon juice
salt and black pepper

Remove the crusts from the bread, then cut a deep square in each slice, leaving a narrow border all the way round. Brush the slices (cut side only) generously with the melted butter and place on a baking tray. Put into a hot oven for 20 minutes or until crisp.

Meanwhile, prepare the sauce. Melt the remaining butter in a medium saucepan and stir in the flour. Cook for a minute, then take off the heat and gradually blend in the milk and reserved juice from the salmon. Cook over a moderate heat, stirring all the time, until the mixture thickens and boils. Reduce the heat and add half the parsley and peas. Flake the salmon into quite large chunks, removing any bones as you do so. Add to the sauce with the quartered eggs and fold in carefully. Heat gently until piping hot, then season to taste with a little lemon juice, salt and pepper.

Take the croustades out of the oven and transfer to hot plates. Fill with the salmon mixture (don't attempt to keep it within the square, it's bound to spread over the sides) and dust lightly with the remaining parsley. Serve with a crisp green salad.

Serves 4

━ 15 minutes   ▣ 20 minutes   ◕ croustades only

118

Potatoes with Cheese and Ham

If there is no tinned ham on the larder shelf, proceed without it – the result will still be delicious.

4 large potatoes, peeled
1 1-lb (450g) tin cooked ham
3 oz (75g) butter
1 medium onion, peeled and
  thinly sliced

salt and pepper
4 oz (100g) good Cheddar,
  grated

Cut the potatoes into thin, crosswise slices. Take just under half the ham and dice it finely.

Melt 1 oz (25g) of butter in a round, 8-inch (20cm) tin (at least 1 inch/2.5cm deep and preferably non-stick) and sauté the onion until golden brown. Lift out and put to one side. Melt another 1 oz (25g) of butter in the same pan and swirl it round so it coats the sides and bottom evenly. Then arrange a layer of potatoes in the bottom and cook over moderate heat for 10–15 minutes, until nicely browned. Take the pan off the heat and season the potatoes with salt and pepper. Scatter a little onion, cheese and ham over the top, repeating the layers until you get to the top of the tin, and ending with a layer of potatoes. Scatter any remaining cheese over the top and dot with the remaining butter. Cover with foil* and bake in a hot oven (400°F/Gas Mark 6/200°C) for an hour, or until the potatoes feel tender when pierced with a skewer. Take out, loosen round the outside edge with a knife and allow to stand in the tin for 5 minutes. Then put a plate on top of the tin and carefully reverse the galette on to it. Cut into wedges and serve with the remaining ham.

Serves 4

━ 15 minutes   ▣ 25 minutes + 1 hour (oven)   ◕ to *

Peach and Blackberry Crumble

1 8-oz (225g) tin blackberries *or* use fresh or frozen	juice of 1 large lemon
2 14-oz (400g) tins peach slices, well drained of syrup	1/2 teaspoon ground cinnamon

Crumble Topping

4 oz (100g) plain flour	2 oz (50g) soft brown sugar
3 oz (75g) butter	4 oz (100g) crunchy oat cereal

Preheat the oven to 375°F/Gas Mark 5/190°C. Lightly butter a baking or soufflé dish roughly 8 inches (20cm) in diameter and put to one side.

Drain the blackberries of juice (if using frozen ones, make sure they are completely thawed first) and arrange with the peach slices in the prepared dish. Pour over the lemon juice, then sprinkle the cinnamon evenly on top.

Sift the flour into a large bowl and rub in the butter until the mixture resembles coarse breadcrumbs. Blend in the sugar and the oat cereal, then spread over the fruit. Bake in the centre of the preheated oven for 45 minutes or until nicely browned (if it seems to be browning too quickly, cover loosely with foil). Serve warm with natural yogurt or cream.

Serves 6

● 20 minutes   ◉ 45 minutes (oven)

French Apricot Tart

8 oz (225g) frozen puff pastry, thawed	1 small egg, lightly beaten
6 tablespoons apricot jam	2 14-oz (400g) tins apricot halves or slices, drained
2 tablespoons water	1 1/2 oz (40g) granulated sugar
juice of 1 large ripe lemon	

Roll out the pastry to make a large rectangle. Transfer to a dampened baking sheet. Cut off a 1-inch (2.5cm) strip all the way round the outside edge. Make a raised border with it round the outside edge, overlapping the strips at the corners. Mark the border at 1/4-inch (.50cm) intervals with diagonal lines, to seal and decorate. Prick the base all over, then chill.

Meanwhile, melt the apricot jam with the water and lemon juice, whisking over gentle heat until it becomes smooth and syrupy. Sieve, then return to the pan off the heat. Preheat the oven to 425°F/Gas Mark 7/220°C.

When ready to bake the tart, brush the base generously with apricot glaze. Put a little beaten egg on the pastry border (too much will make it burn). Put rows of apricots on top of the glaze, overlapping them slightly, and scatter the sugar evenly on top. Place in the middle of the oven for 15 minutes, then bake for 15–25 more minutes at 400°F/Gas Mark 6/200°C, until the pastry is crisp and nicely browned. (Check that it doesn't brown too quickly.) Warm up the glaze slightly, then use to brush the border, the apricots and any gaps between them. Cool to lukewarm and serve (or serve cold).

Serves 6

● 15 minutes   ◉ 5 minutes + 40 minutes (oven)

Basic Recipes

Basic Shortcrust Pastry
(for Savoury Dishes)

6 oz (175g) plain flour
pinch of salt

3 oz (75g) butter *or* half lard,
half butter
3–4 tablespoons iced water

Sift the flour and salt into a large mixing bowl. Rub in the butter until the mixture resembles coarse breadcrumbs. Add the iced water and mix with a knife or fork until most of it holds together. Then press together quickly with your fingertips and shape into a ball. Wrap in greaseproof paper and chill for at least 30 minutes.

Basic Shortcrust Pastry
(for Sweet Dishes)

6 oz (175g) plain flour
pinch of salt
3 oz (75g) butter

1 level tablespoon castor sugar
1 egg yolk
2 tablespoons iced water

Sift the flour and salt into a large mixing bowl. Rub in the butter, then mix in the sugar. Blend the egg yolk and water together and add enough to bind the dry ingredients together. Shape into a ball, wrap tightly in a large piece of greaseproof paper and chill for 30 minutes.

Rich Shortcrust Pastry
(for Savoury Dishes)

6 oz (175g) plain flour
pinch of salt
4 oz (100g) butter

1 egg yolk
2–3 tablespoons iced water

Sift the flour and salt into a large mixing bowl. Rub in the butter until the mixture resembles breadcrumbs. Mix the yolk with the water and tip over the dry ingredients. Mix quickly with a knife or fork until most of it holds together. Then shape quickly into a ball, knead lightly, and wrap tightly in a large piece of greaseproof paper. Chill for at least 30 minutes.

Crisp French Pastry
(*Pâte Sucrée*)

6 oz (175g) plain flour
pinch of salt
3 oz (75g) butter, at room
  temperature

2 oz (50g) castor sugar
2 standard egg yolks
a drop of vanilla essence

Sift the flour and salt on to a clean, cold work surface or marble slab. Make a large well in the centre and in it put the butter and sugar, then the egg yolks and vanilla. Using the fingertips of one hand, work these last four ingredients together (use a 'pecking' motion) until you have a soft, smooth paste. Then, with fingers or the edge of a palette knife, gradually work in the flour from around the sides until it has all been incorporated and the dough is pliant. Wrap in greaseproof paper and chill for at least 30 minutes.

Wholemeal Pastry

6 oz (175g) wholewheat flour
  (plain or self-raising)
large pinch of salt

1¹/₂ oz (40g) butter
1¹/₂ oz (40g) lard
3–5 tablespoons iced water

Sift the flour and salt into a large mixing bowl, then tip in the bran that remains in the sieve. Rub in the butter and lard until the mixture resembles breadcrumbs. Add the iced water and mix quickly with a knife or fork until it leaves the sides of the bowl clean. Shape into a ball, knead lightly, then roll out. Chill for at least 30 minutes before baking.

Wholewheat Crêpes

¹/₂ lb (225g) wholewheat flour
¹/₂ teaspoon salt
³/₄ pint (425ml) milk (or milk
  and water mixed)

2 eggs, lightly beaten
1 oz (25g) melted butter

Sift the flour and salt into a mixing bowl, tipping in the bran that remains at the end. Make a well in the centre and gradually blend in the beaten eggs and milk. Finally, blend in the melted butter. Allow the batter to rest for at least half an hour before using.

Makes 12–14 small crêpes

Wheatmeal Pastry

3 oz (75g) plain flour
3 oz (75g) wholewheat flour
large pinch of salt

1¹/₂ oz (40g) butter
1¹/₂ oz (40g) lard
3–5 tablespoons iced water

Sift the flours and salt into a large mixing bowl, then tip in the bran that remains in the sieve. Rub in the butter and lard until the mixture resembles breadcrumbs. Add the iced water and mix in quickly with a knife or fork until it leaves the sides of the bowl clean. Shape into a ball and knead lightly until smooth. Roll out and use to line flan or tartlet tins. Then chill for 30 minutes before baking.

Crêpes

6 oz (175g) plain flour
good pinch of salt
1 dessertspoon sugar (only if
  the filling is sweet)
2 large eggs

1 egg yolk
8 fl oz milk
7 fl oz (200ml) water
1¹/₂ oz (40g) melted butter

Sift the flour and salt (with the sugar, if used) into a large mixing bowl. Make a well in the middle, then tip in the eggs and yolk, lightly beaten together. Gradually draw in the flour from around the sides until you have a smooth paste. Gradually whisk in the milk and water until you have a smooth batter. Finally whisk in the melted butter. Allow the batter to rest for at least half an hour before using.

Makes 10–12 small crêpes

Mayonnaise

2 egg yolks
1 level teaspoon pale French
  mustard
salt
$^1/_2$ pint (275ml) good olive oil
  or olive and vegetable oil
  mixed

1 tablespoon white wine
  vinegar
good squeeze of lemon juice
white pepper

Make sure that all the ingredients are at room temperature, then put the yolks into a small bowl. Mix in the mustard with a little salt, then whisk in the oil – drop by drop – until it begins to thicken. Then pour the oil in a thin, steady stream, whisking all the time. When it becomes thick, whisk in the vinegar. When all the oil has been incorporated, add a good squeeze of lemon juice and season to taste with salt and pepper. (If the mayonnaise becomes too thick – thin with a little hot water.)

Alternatively, the mayonnaise can be made in a food processor or liquidizer – pouring the oil through the opening in the cap, with the machine on.

Makes about $^1/_2$ pint (275ml)

Yogurt Dressing

$^1/_2$ teaspoon dry mustard
$^1/_2$ teaspoon castor sugar
$^1/_2$ teaspoon salt
1 level tablespoon flour
2 tablespoons white wine or
  cider vinegar

3 tablespoons milk
3 tablespoons water
2 egg yolks
2 tablespoons melted butter
5 oz (150ml) natural yogurt
white pepper

Mix the mustard, sugar, salt and flour together in a small bowl. Gradually blend in the vinegar, milk, water, egg yolks and melted butter. Put over a pan of gently simmering water and whisk until the mixture thickens. Take off the heat and whisk in the yogurt. Season with pepper and more salt if needed. Allow to cool completely, then store in a screw-top jar in the refrigerator.

Makes $^1/_2$ pint (275ml)

Chicken Stock

1 oz (25g) butter
1 rasher unsmoked bacon, trimmed and diced
1 large onion, peeled and chopped
2 large carrots, peeled and sliced
1 large leek, roughly chopped
large stalk of celery, roughly chopped
bouquet garni (bay leaf, sprig of thyme, parsley)
8 peppercorns
salt
1 chicken carcass
water

Melt the butter in a very large saucepan and add the bacon dice. Cook until the fat begins to run, then add the onion and cook until it becomes soft and transparent. Add the remaining vegetables, cover with a piece of buttered paper and 'sweat' for about 10 minutes. Remove the paper, add the *bouquet garni*, peppercorns and a good sprinkling of salt. Put the chicken carcass on top and just cover with water. Bring up to the boil, then reduce the heat and simmer uncovered for 2–3 hours. Strain, discarding the carcass and vegetables, and pour the stock back into the pan. Allow to cool, then skim off the fat and adjust the seasoning. Refrigerate or freeze.

Makes about 2 pints (1.1 litres)

Beef Stock

3 lbs (1.5 kilos) beef bones
a little butter or beef dripping
2 large onions, quartered (skin left on)
2 large leeks, roughly chopped
2 large carrots, scrubbed and chopped
2 stalks of celery, roughly chopped
handful of mushroom stalks
bouquet garni (bay leaf, sprig of thyme, parsley)
8 peppercorns
salt
3–4 pints (1.7–2.3 litres) water

Put the beef bones in a very large deep saucepan and brown gently for 15–20 minutes. Then add a small amount of butter or beef dripping to the pan with all the vegetables. Cook for a further 20 minutes or until the vegetables are soft and lightly coloured. Add the *bouquet garni*, peppercorns and a good sprinkling of salt. Pour in the water and bring up to the boil. Then reduce the heat and simmer for about 4 hours. Strain the stock, discarding the bones and vegetables, then return to the pan. Allow to cool, then skim off the fat. Taste for seasoning and adjust if necessary.

Makes about 1¹/₂ pints (850ml)

Useful Lists

Meals in 15 minutes
Field Mushroom Croustades
Tomatoes with Guacamole
Tomato and Mozzarella Salad
Liver with Sage and Bacon
Devilled Lamb Chops

Ham with Cider and Raisin Sauce
Kippers with Scrambled Egg
Omelette Bonne Femme
Soufflé Omelette

Meals within half an hour
Stir-fried Cabbage with Fennel
  and Sausage
Ragoût of Lettuce, Mushrooms
  and Peas
New Potato and Frankfurter
  Salad
Italian Salad with Tuna and
  Peppers
Chicken Salad with Brazil Nuts
  and Grapes
Turkey Waldorf
Salade Niçoise
English Apple, Date and
  Asparagus Salad
Curried Turkey Salad
Chinese Chicken with Nuts and
  Celery
Chicken with Broccoli, Beans and
  Red Pepper
Chicken Livers with Spinach and
  Bacon
Beef with Leeks, Beans and
  Spring Onions

Kidneys with Creamy Mustard
  Sauce
Veal or Pork with Lemon
Pork Chops with Gruyère and
  Mustard
Grilled Ham with Melon
Cod with Garlic Mayonnaise
Monkfish with Bacon
Moules Marinière
Prawns with Lemon and Garlic
Pipérade
Mumbled Eggs
Molly-coddled Eggs with Leeks
Eggs in Bathrobes
Eggs Benedicta
Spanish Tortilla
Omelette Arnold Bennett
Tagliatelle with Mushrooms,
  Bacon and Garlic
Pasta with Blue Cheese and
  Walnuts
Fettucine with Peas and Ham
Vegetable Fried Rice

Meals within 1 hour
Ricotta and Vegetable Custard
Winter Vegetable Purée
Cauliflower with Curry Cream
  Sauce
Sausage and Toasted Cauliflower
Honeyed Chicken with Meaux
  Mustard
Chicken Maryland
Turkey in Green Waistcoats

Schmaltzburgers
Lamb with Rice, Spices and Nuts
Pork with Cider and Spices
Pork with Parsnip Purée
Porkers with Red Cabbage
Haddock with Sesame Seed
  Crumbs
Little Pots of Smoked Haddock
Cod with Cider and Mushrooms

Red Mullet with Fennel
Trout in a Paper Bag
Atlantic Gratinée
Salmon Kedgeree
Cheese Soufflé
Spinach Soufflé
Baked Eggs Savoyarde

Ambushed Eggs
Tortellini with Creamy Tomato
  Sauce
Spaghetti for Crowds
Creole Rice with Prawns
Chicken Cobbler
Crespolini

Dishes which cook for 1–2 hours
Scalloped Potatoes with Ham
The Shoemaker's Chicken
Spiced Chicken
Butter Roast Chicken
Chicken in a Pot
Carpetbag Steak
Beef Stew with Orange

Spring Lamb Stew
Epigrams of Lamb
Veal with Soured Cream and
  Mushrooms
Creamy Veal with Carrots
Virginia Baked Ham
Cannelloni

Recipes which can be prepared 1–2 hours ahead
The Priest Has Fainted
Potatoes in Dinner Jackets
Stir-fried Cabbage with Fennel
  and Sausage
New Potato and Frankfurter
  Salad
Italian Salad with Tuna and
  Peppers
Chicken Salad with Brazil Nuts
  and Grapes
Turkey Waldorf
Salade Niçoise
Californian Coleslaw
Carrot Salad with Nuts and
  Raisins
Winter Cabbage Salad
Poulet Grand'mère
Honeyed Chicken with Meaux
  Mustard
Trinidad Chicken
Turkey in Green Waistcoats
Carpetbag Steak
Beef Teriyaki

Lamb with Mint Butter (mint
  butter only)
Devilled Lamb Chops
Pork with Cider and Spices
Pork Boulangère
Porkers with Red Cabbage (red
  cabbage only)
Grilled Ham with Melon (sauce
  only)
Haddock with Sesame Seed
  Crumbs
Monkfish with Bacon
Red Mullet with Fennel
Trout in a Paper Bag
The Two Sisters' Soufflé
Tagliatelle with Mushrooms,
  Bacon and Garlic (sauce only)
Tortellini with Creamy Tomato
  Sauce (sauce only)
Wholemeal Vegetable Pasties
Crispy Pancakes with Ratatouille
  Filling

Recipes that can be prepared the day before
All the soups
Baked Aubergines with Tomatoes
  and Cheese
Scalloped Potatoes with Ham
Gratin of Potatoes, Leeks and
  Ham

Stuffed Onions
New Potato Salad with Celery
  and Ham
Tabbouleh
Brown Rice Salad
Chicken with Leeks and Bacon

The Shoemaker's Chicken
Chicken with Marmalade
  Marinade
Chicken Maryland
Tandoori Chicken
Miss Moffat's Cottage Pie
Spiced Chicken
Moussaka
Spring Lamb Stew
Veal with Soured Cream and
  Mushrooms
Creamy Veal with Carrots
Sweet and Sour Pork
Pork with Barbecue Sauce (sauce
  only)
Ham with Cider and Raisin Sauce
  (sauce only)
Mackerel with Rhubarb Purée
  (purée only)
Little Pots of Smoked Haddock
Cod with Cider and Mushrooms
Cod with Garlic Mayonnaise
  (mayonnaise only)

Atlantic Gratinée
Salmon Kedgeree (sauce only)
Molly-coddled Eggs with Leeks
Spaghetti for Crowds (sauce only)
Baked Macaroni with Asparagus
  and Ham
Lasagne
Cannelloni
Watercress and Walnut Quiche
Quiche Paysanne
Spring Onion Quiche
Spinach and Cottage Cheese
  Quiche
Leek and Ham Pie
Beef Jalousie
Humble Pie
Beefsteak, Kidney and Mushroom
  Pie
Fisherman's Pie
Crespolini

Recipes which are very quick to prepare

Roast Jerusalem Artichokes with
  Leeks and Bacon
Frizzy Salad with Bacon
Chicken with Marmalade
  Marinade
Tandoori Chicken
Spiced Chicken
Butter Roast Chicken
Chicken in a Pot
Trinidad Chicken
Beef Teriyaki
Beef with Leeks and Spring
  Onions
Liver with Sage and Bacon
Devilled Lamb Chops
Kidneys in Baked Potatoes
Pork Boulangère

Pork Chops with Gruyère and
  Mustard
Pork with Barbecue Sauce
Grilled Ham with Melon
Mackerel with Rhubarb Purée
Monkfish with Bacon
Moules Marinière
Prawns with Lemon and Garlic
The Two Sisters' Soufflé
Pipérade
Spanish Tortilla
Omelette Arnold Bennett
Omelette Bonne Femme
Soufflé Omelette
Pasta with Blue Cheese and
  Walnuts
Pissaladière

Good supper-party dishes

Chicken with Leeks and Bacon
Poulet Grand'mere
Chinese Chicken with Nuts and
  Celery
Spiced Chicken
Chicken in a Pot

Turkey in Green Waistcoats
Veal with Soured Cream and
  Mushrooms
Creamy Veal with Carrots
Sweet and Sour Pork
Spring Lamb Stew

Moussaka
Lasagne
Cannelloni
Baked Macaroni with Asparagus
  and Ham

Chicken Cobbler
Fisherman's Pie

Cooking for crowds

Potatoes in Dinner Jackets
Soufflé Potatoes
Winter Cabbage Salad
Californian Coleslaw
Tandoori Chicken
Chilli con Carne
Schmaltzburgers
Pork with Barbecue Sauce
Virginia Baked Ham
Lasagne

Spaghetti for Crowds
Baked Macaroni with Asparagus
  and Ham
Pilau Rice
Saffron Rice with Nuts and
  Raisins
Chicken Cobbler
Presto Pizza
Chicago-style Pizza

Children's favourites

Basil's Chicken Soup
Sweetcorn Chowder
Whizzo Carrot Soup
Gratin of Ham, Leeks and New
  Potatoes
Sausage and Toasted Cauliflower
New Potato and Frankfurter
  Salad
Carrot Salad with Nuts and
  Raisins
Chicken with Marmalade
  Marinade
Chicken Maryland
Butter Roast Chicken

Miss Moffat's Cottage Pie
Schmaltzburgers
Pork with Barbecue Sauce
Chicken Cobbler
Haddock with Sesame Seed
  Crumbs
The Two Sisters' Soufflé
Wholemeal Vegetable Pasties
Presto Pizza
Chicago-style Pizza
Hot Oscars
The Mars Mousse
Boston Baked Beans
Butterscotch Brownies

Slimmers' suppers

Vegetable Linguine with Spring
  Onion Sauce
Tomato and Mozzarella Salad
  with Basil
Salad Niçoise
Chicken with Broccoli, Beans and
  Red Pepper

Tandoori Chicken
Liver with Sage and Bacon
Monkfish with Bacon
Prawns with Lemon and Garlic
Trout in a Paper Bag
Soufflé Omelette
Omelette Arnold Bennett

Index